Second-Grade Reading Growth Spurt

Lucy Calkins and Shanna Schwartz

Photography by Peter Cunningham

Illustrations by Marjorie Martinelli

HEINEMANN ◆ PORTSMOUTH, NH

To Lila, Thank you for all the book marathons, past and future. Reading with you is my favorite way to spend an evening.—Shanna

To Adele, with brimming admiration for the way you fuse a focus on rigor with an attention to joy. Thanks for leading a school that illustrates child-centered teaching at its best, and thanks for helping us feel as if your school is ours as well.—Lucy

Heinemann
361 Hanover Street
Portsmouth, NH 03801–3912
www.heinemann.com

Offices and agents throughout the world

The authors and publisher wish to thank those who have generously given permission to reprint borrowed material:

Katie Woo Has the Flu © 2012 by Picture Window Books, an imprint by Capstone. All rights reserved.

Those Darn Squirrels, by Adam Rubin. Houghton Mifflin Harcourt, 2008. Used by permission of Houghton Mifflin Harcourt.

Mercy Watson to the Rescue. Text Copyright © 2005 by Kate DiCamillo. Illustrations Copyright © 2005 by Chris Van Dusen. Reproduced by permission of the publisher, Candlewick Press.

Materials by Kaeden Books and Lee & Low Books, appearing throughout the primary Reading Units of Study series, are reproduced by generous permission of the publishers. A detailed list of credits is available in the Grade 2 online resources.

Cataloging-in-Publication data is on file with the Library of Congress.

ISBN-13: 978-0-325-07707-9

Series editorial team: Anna Gratz Cockerille, Karen Kawaguchi, Tracy Wells, Felicia O'Brien, Debra Doorack, Jean Lawler, Marielle Palombo, and Sue Paro
Production: Elizabeth Valway, David Stirling, and Abigail Heim
Cover and interior designs: Jenny Jensen Greenleaf
Photography: Peter Cunningham
Illustrations: Marjorie Martinelli
Composition: Publishers' Design and Production Services, Inc.
Manufacturing: Steve Bernier

Printed in the United States of America on acid-free paper
19 18 17 16 15   PAH   2 3 4 5

Acknowledgments

HAVE YOU EVER MADE maple syrup? Just as the winter snows begin to melt, you hang buckets from maple trees, and then half a day later, pour that bucket full of sap into a giant pot, where it boils for days until at long last you pour what seems like a tablespoon of maple syrup into special bottles for syrup. It is the volume of sap—and of work, too—that goes into making that beautiful sweet syrup that impresses us most.

The book looks slim now, in contrast to the months of drafts. We wrote our way into a new level of clarity about methods of teaching. We wrote our way toward a close attentiveness to reading development.

Although the two of us worked long into the nights and through every weekend, we didn't come close to writing this alone. When Project staff works on books, it's always been the case that the shoemakers—the authors—have access to elves who come into the workshop while the shoemaker is sleeping and move the work forward. In our community, the elves work on conferring and small-group sections, add in coaching text and getting ready sections, rewrite confusing parts of minilessons, and suggest mid-workshop teaching or a share. On this book, one elf came into the book almost every evening, and that is Julie Steinberg, and we thank her. We had other elves as well. Thanks especially to Julia Mooney, Annemarie Johnson, Beth Moore, and Taryn Vanderburg. We know you drew on your brilliant work with young readers to help us make sure that every page of this book is just-right—thank you.

We are both especially grateful to Amanda Hartman. Those of you who know our videos and books know Amanda. You have a sense for how precious her professional companionship is to us. Amanda is able to invite people into learning, to provide the right balance of support and of space. We love, too, the way you write with a directness and an energy that makes it impossible not to want to teach your words to a class full of seven-year-olds.

Special thanks also go to Kathy Collins, who has for decades helped us learn from young children and their teachers. We've so relished her reminders that the best-laid plans will get upturned and teaching involves being ready for anything. Kathy, thank you for keeping us leaning forward to learn.

Of course, we could not have written this book without the wisdom of Joe Yukish. Joe's encyclopedic knowledge of reading development informs everything we do and keeps us focused on how children grow stronger reading skills.

We thank Mary Ann Mustac, who brings grace, professionalism, creative energy, and class to our organization. We thank Sara Johnson, who is a wizard of all things visual.

We thank Carmen Fariña, Chancellor of New York City schools, who has shone a spotlight on second grade, pointing out to the entire city that this is a year of amazing growth for kids. Once upon a time, people thought of second grade as an extension of first, a time to consolidate the gains of grade one before the push of grade three. Chancellor Fariña is pointing out everywhere that second-grade teachers carry an especially big responsibility, as they bring every child along and launch all kids into the world of chapter books.

The extraordinary thing about these books is that they tap the finest talents and represent the highest standards of literally two score of people. While we worked away, a team at Heinemann worked with equal fervor. We're endlessly grateful to our editor, Sue Paro, and the talented Beth Moore, both of whom helped this book to be the absolute best it could be. Because this book was one of the first in the K–2 series, it asked a lot of you, and we're grateful for your hard work and care. Thanks also to Anna Gratz Cockerille who did a yeoman's job to keep everything moving along smoothly and in sync throughout this project.

—Shanna and Lucy

Contents

BEND III Paying Close Attention to Authors

Read-Aloud and Shared Reading

An Orientation to the Unit

REMEMBER HOW, WHEN YOU were little, time moved more slowly and summers seemed to stretch forever? For your youngsters, the time between the end of last year and the start of this one will have seemed very long indeed. You may want to begin your reading workshop by celebrating your children's growth. "Second-graders, you are all becoming so grown up! So many changes! How many of you got taller this summer?" Around the meeting area, children will spring up to show you how tall they've become, and you'll admire their growth spurt. "Growing up means you get to do more cool stuff, right? Are any of you getting new bedtimes? Getting to watch new shows? Yes? Wait, wait, I have a better question. Are any of you getting new chores?"

Soon, of course, you'll turn towards what becomes the theme for the unit and, in a sense, for the year: "Readers, today I want to teach you that reading, also, changes as you get older. Second-grade readers don't only get to read *harder* and *longer* books, they also get to be in charge of their own reading. They get to choose not only *what* they are going to read but also *how* they are going to read."

To cement children's expectations for a year in which they'll grow and grow and *grow* as readers, you'll remind them of that beanstalk in the beloved tale, "Jack and the Beanstalk," explaining that there are scientists—researchers, really—who study young kids as readers, and they say that in the one year—second grade—children grow like that beanstalk.

The truth is that second grade is a year when kids' newfound reading powers allow them to do powerful new things as readers, and above all, their reading skills allow them to think. Whereas first-graders are often consumed with breaking the code—reading the words—by second grade, children need to do some serious thinking about books. While second-graders continue to do important word-solving work, they must also develop automaticity with print so they can read with the rhythms of natural speech. As second-grade fluency skyrockets, readers will read faster too—going from 50 words per minute to 100. Many second-graders begin the year reading Henry and Mudge books and leave reading Magic Tree House books. To make this kind of growth, readers need to construct meaning and to understand how longer, more complicated stories are held together.

This move from a "little-kid" focus on print to a "big-kid" focus on meaning is a challenging one, and yet it is necessary if your children are to develop into avid readers. This unit is written to create the mindset that will allow them to rally around the hard work of outgrowing themselves as readers.

In the first bend of the unit, you point out to readers that in order to grow, they need to take charge of their growth. They need to choose not only *what* to read but also *how* to read. This portion of the unit, then, highlights the importance of goals and of that magical combination of fluency and comprehension. Once your readers have taken charge of their reading, you'll let them know that grown-up readers don't wait around for others to help them with the hard parts, which then leads into the mantra of Bend II: "Now that you are in second grade, you need to roll up your sleeves and work hard to solve tricky words." This second bend will remind readers that if they want to read well, they'll need to be able to figure out even the hardest words on their own. You'll say, "When second-grade readers come to a tricky word, they don't just say, 'Help me, help me!' Instead, second-graders roll up their sleeves and get to work! They draw on *everything* they already know to figure out that hard word." In Bend III, readers learn to read like writers. You'll start by letting your children know that every time they react in their books—every time they giggle or gasp or sigh—it's because the author did something special in the writing to evoke that reaction. Each time they have a reaction, they can ask themselves, "How did the author do that?"

The three bends, then, focus on fluency and comprehension, word solving, and reading like a writer and making reading-writing connections.

THE INTERSECTION OF READING DEVELOPMENT AND THIS UNIT

Second grade is the year when you teach kids what it means to read, helping them understand that reading well is not just saying the words, but that it's noticing how an author crafts a book, mulling over the lesson the story teaches, using reading to grow knowledge about volcanoes and Mars, race cars and ponies. For the first time, the books that were always "wait-until-you-are-older" books are now within reach. Seven-year-olds needn't recruit a grown-up to read them that book about sharks, nor must they wait a year to read that Pokémon book with the stickers on the pages. And the picture books that were read to them earlier—*The Three Billy Goats Gruff, Caps for Sale*, and the rest—are now books that second-graders can read to little kids! These youngsters finally have the reading skills to explore the full range of genres. And explore they do, as they gallop between joke books, how-to books, graphic chapter books, mysteries, biographies, historical fiction, baby fantasy books, choose-your-own-adventure books—the works.

Of course, none of that is true for *all* second-graders, because the other defining characteristic of this grade is that you'll have some kids who read at level I and below and do one kind of reading work, while others read at level J and above and do a whole different kind of reading work.

No matter what, however, second-graders are moving into books that are longer, and therefore it will be important for you to teach them to retell—and to do so in ways that help them put the pieces of longer texts together. For children who are reading at level G/H/I, the emphasis on retelling will be combined with encouragement to retell by chunks, not by pages. If Rosie dropped her plate on one page, stamped her foot on another, and screamed aloud on a third, you'll teach readers of that book to be able to say one sentence about all those activities and all those pages: Rosie got mad. Teaching readers to synthesize is important because it allows them to hold on to—to cumulate—the text. Of course, your students who are reading at even higher levels (and some of the readers working at level G/H/I) will find it helpful to retell stories by thinking of story structure and by thinking who the characters are, what they are like, what problems they encounter, and how they respond to them. That is, story structure becomes a way for your more experienced second-grade readers to retell, putting the pages of their now-longer books together.

Another way in which you will help all your readers pull their now-longer texts together is by teaching them to think about how their books click together and especially to think about how the ending fits with the larger story. When readers are moving through the more emergent stages of reading, they come to expect that the end of a book will have a twist or make a joke. Now the endings are more apt to cohere with the rest of the story—they may solve a problem or reflect back on an earlier aspect of the text. This poses important new work for readers to do. For example, in the story *The Little Red Hen*, when all of the animals are ready at the end to help the Little Hen eat her freshly baked bread, that ending is utterly related to the fact that throughout the story, each of these animals refused to help the Little Red Hen with the many steps of growing, harvesting, and milling the wheat that she finally used to bake the bread. That is, making sense of this ending requires children to think about how all of the parts of the text fit together. Often when an ending reflects back on the story, it throws light on details that might have been overlooked all along. This often happens when a reader reaches the solution to the mysteries that second-graders love—such as those about Cam Jansen and Nate the Great.

When you teach students to think about how the endings of their stories relate back to the whole story, the important part of this is not really those endings at all. The important thing is that when readers can synthesize and summarize what is happening in the story, this sets them up to be able to do inferential thinking, which becomes more and more important as children progress up the levels. Oftentimes when teachers say that a reader of early chapter books doesn't make "good" inferences, the real problem is not the quality of inferential thought, but rather the fact that the reader hasn't actually grasped the storyline as a whole. Usually the problem is that the reader has been trying to hold on to every little thing in a story, and therefore ends up holding on to nothing. So the instruction you will give your second-graders in this unit—instruction that aims to help them see how their stories click together and how the endings fit with the rest of the story—is all key.

Of course, fluency plays a big part in helping second-graders pull together the longer books they are now reading, and second grade itself is the year for fluency development. Some of your readers—those who are at reading level I and below—will read in such a way that patches of a book sound fluent. With the right feedback, those readers can get a vision for the sound of fluent reading. Meanwhile, the readers who are working at level J and above can learn, with coaching, that their intonation can reflect the content of the story more when they pay closer attention to punctuation and to a character's traits and feelings.

In order for children to practice reading with fluency, they'll need to be holding just-right books (or to have lots of support in the just-a-bit-too-hard books), and so your work in this first bend will involve assessing children as quickly as possible. You'll listen in as children read, and you'll take running records, checking if the child reads word-by-word, or in more fluent three- to four-word phrases. For students who are reading at grade level (I/J/K), you'll expect this kind of fluency to be in place or to emerge as the children rub off the summer rust. Of course, there will be some children for whom phrasing is still a struggle. For these children, cementing their command of familiar high-frequency words can help them scoop up more words at a time. You will also want to encourage them to reread often, working toward better phrasing with each successive read-through of the text.

Accuracy will play a part here as well, although reading will go underground for many of your children, so their miscues will be less obvious to you. That is, most of them will be reading silently now. Still, you will watch them get stuck on many hard words. You can tie the work on word solving to your overall message, reminding kids that, "Sometimes reading is not so easy. You have to roll up your sleeves, say to yourself, 'I can do this!' and get to work!" You can later say, "Here's the thing: when you read longer books, you also end up reading longer or more complicated words. Really! You are going to find words like these in your books," and you can point to words like *genius* from *Those Darn Squirrels* by Adam Rubin, *ferret* in Stan Kirby's *Captain Awesome to the Rescue*, and *mesmerizing* from *Mrs. Jafee Is Daffy!* by Dan Gutman. When teaching your second-graders that they need to roll up their sleeves and get to work, you'll be teaching your readers who are working with texts at level I and below to work on the sounds that are in the middle of words and on compound words, and the readers who are reading at level J and above to tackle multisyllabic words.

Finally, the conferring and small-group work in this book is different because your children are second-graders now. In kindergarten and first grade, teachers in your school probably tended to confer and lead small groups in which a large portion of time revolved around having children reading aloud to research and coach their reading process. This year, you will now spend more of your conferring and small-group time (at least with readers on benchmark) supporting comprehension. For this unit, a fiction unit, you'll be asking readers to tell you about the characters: What do they want? What are the big things that have happened so far? How does that ending fit with the rest of the story? What do you think the character learned? As you move into the second part of the unit, you'll want to get guided reading and other small-group teaching going.

Based on your assessments, you'll probably notice students who need support with a variety of early transitional reading skills (*transitional readers* typically refers to readers in levels I/J/K/L). For example, some children may need support with their high-frequency word knowledge. By the time children reach level L, most have about 200 high-frequency words under their belts. For children who need to expand their bank of high-frequency words, you can teach a quick little routine. First, teach children to *look* at a word, noticing how many letters it has and its shape, and then to *read* the word out loud. Next, they'll *spell* the word, perhaps chanting it several times, and then they'll *write* it. Finally, children will *look* at and *read* the word again to be sure they wrote the word correctly. Let the group go through this routine with each word and then independently read a book or two from their baggies, pushing to read known words automatically. Chapter 11, "Word Study," in *A Guide to the Reading Workshop, Primary Grades* will help.

Learning to monitor for understanding when reading words can also be a challenge for second-graders. Often their books will now contain unfamiliar vocabulary or familiar words that are being used in ways they don't understand. To prepare for this teaching, look through a small group of readers' books and mark a few pages with words that you anticipate will be tough for children to understand. Then pull them together and say, "Sometimes, words you know can have a whole new meaning when used in different ways in books. Even when you can *say* a word, it's important to stop and check that you understand what it *means*. Right now I would like you to read the books that I marked up and, when you get to a page with a Post-it, slow down, look for a word that might mean something new, and sketch what you think it means on your Post-it!"

It will be critical to make reading as social as possible this year. Second-graders are, in a way, like a young version of adolescents. Just as this is the age when they need to push away adults, saying, "I can do it on my own!" This is also the age when they want to be with their peers. Throughout this unit and this year, you'll use partners, and eventually clubs, to invite readers to share their opinions, to debate with each other, to figure out things together, to prove their points—that is, to collaborate.

OVERVIEW

This unit progresses through three parts. The first bend launches the year and gets readers working toward the big work of reading with fluency, stamina, and comprehension. The second bend recruits students to work on tackling hard words. The final bend invites readers to use what they are learning in writing to help them think more deeply in reading.

Bend I: Taking Charge of Reading

In this bend, children learn that growing up doesn't just mean getting taller; it also means growing to be stronger readers. You'll tell children that stronger readers make lots of decisions as they read; they decide how their reading will sound, how much they will read, and how to make sure their reading makes sense. As children begin to read longer texts, it will be important for them to synthesize chunks of the text in order to hold on to what is happening in the stories. This work starts when you ask students whether they learned to do sneak peeks of their books in first grade. Whether they learned this or not, you'll show them that second-graders preview in more encompassing ways. You'll teach them that second-grade readers don't just get ready to read by looking at the cover of a book and thinking, "What will this book be about?" No! Second-grade readers look at the back of the book and the table of contents, too, if there is one, and they read a little bit of the first page. Reading the blurb and studying the table of contents helps readers predict what the characters might want, what might get in the way, and how the story will move from the problem to the solution. That instruction may seem to be about previewing, but really, of course, it supports the larger work of helping students to synthesize.

During the first days of school, you'll rally your students towards reading more fluently by pointing out that when children preview texts and begin to read them, they think, "How does this book *want* to be read?" Is this a funny "ha-ha" book? A sad, mournful book? Within a few days, you'll come back to this tip, pointing out that readers try to bring out the feelings in a book. You'll say, "Some parts of books are written to be read in a soft, sweet voice, like this, 'Once upon a time in a land far, far away, lived a little old woman . . . ,' and some pages are written to be roared, like this, 'I'll huff and I'll puff and I'll *blow* your house down!'"

Previewing will soon support students' work in reviewing and retelling. A favorite minilesson involves you confessing to children that after teaching them to put their words together and read smoothly, you found yourself sleepless. "When I lay in bed, I started to worry. So I got out of bed, went over to my desk, found a pen and a Post-it, and wrote myself a reminder to be sure to tell you something. You ready?" Then you will pull a well-folded Post-it out of your pocket and read aloud, "Readers need to be careful not to get going, faster and faster, so they forget to *think* about the story." You go on to teach them that they can keep tabs by stopping to make sure they can retell the events in order.

Of course, part of your teaching during this first bend will support establishing a well-managed reading workshop. This will be a particular challenge because you'll be conducting running records, while also helping readers to get into the routines of a well-oiled reading workshop. We'll provide lots of tips about how to manage the comings and goings, the materials and the time, in your reading workshop, and also about how to make conducting running records as efficient as it can be.

Before you move on to Bend II, hopefully your readers will all have been assessed and partnerships established.

Bend II: Working Hard to Solve Tricky Words

In the second bend, you'll teach children new strategies for word solving quickly and independently. As part of this, children will apply what they are learning in word study about prefixes, suffixes, vowel teams, and vocabulary to their independent reading work. You will convey that reading won't make sense unless they read with accuracy, stopping when something doesn't sound right and drawing on their repertoire of strategies to correct their miscue. Children will learn the importance of being flexible, persistent, independent word solvers; as *second*-grade readers, they cannot rely on others when their reading doesn't make sense. They have to identify and fix their own mistakes.

You'll begin by reminding children of the growth they have made this year as readers: "Earlier, we talked about all the ways that second-graders grow like beanstalks! You have later bedtimes. You get to watch new shows. And reading, too, has changed. You've already grown as readers. Now you each have a brand new reading book baggie to hold books—books that you get to choose all by yourself!" Lean in to create a drumroll for the new work of this bend: "The thing is, you don't just grow automatically. You have to work hard to grow. Sometimes reading is not so easy. You have to roll up your sleeves, say to yourself, 'I can do this!' and get to work!" Then explain that during this bend, children will need to work hard to become independent, determined problem solvers, especially as the words in their books become longer and harder to understand.

After this first session, you'll point out that some words are so tricky that using just one strategy won't help. "Readers, can any of you pat your head and rub your stomach at the same time?" you'll say. Then you'll use this invitation to illustrate the fact that it's not easy to do two things at once. You'll remind readers that even though it's hard, it is useful to use more than one strategy at a time when word solving, encouraging them to draw on all that they have learned to solve tricky words in their books, and to search multiple sources of information (MSV), thinking about what's happening in the story or picture while looking through the whole word, part-by-part.

Over the course of the second bend, you'll build a bridge between word study and reading workshop. You might start by having children notice the prefixes and suffixes in big, long words that they have learned during word study time. Show children that when they chunk words, some of the chunks (the prefixes and suffixes they know) can be read in a snap, which will make it easier to solve the whole word. This will also reinforce the importance of reading words part-by-part.

On another day, you'll bring word study materials and sorts into your mini-lesson. You'll call your readers to the rug saying, "Let's set up our white boards to do some long vowel work. At the top of your board, will you please draw a line down the middle, and write the word *beach* at the top on one side, and *head* on the other?" Then you can invite children to sort a group of words all containing the *ea* vowel team. You'll help children see that rules about vowel teams (such as the adage, "when two vowels go a-walkin', the first one does the talkin'") don't always work, so above all children need to be flexible as they read. Sometimes the letters *ea* represent a long *e* sound (as in *beach* and *teach*), while other times they represent a short *e* sound (as in *breath* and *bread*). You can explain this work, adding, "Look at this! Sometimes the first vowel doesn't do the talkin'! You have to watch out for those tricky vowel teams. Every time you see two vowels together, you can think to yourself, 'Hey, I know you, you tricky vowels—and you're *not* going to trick me!'"

Although you will devote some of your conferring time to supporting the work of the bend, the start of a second bend is also traditionally a time to lead guided reading groups—and now, at the start of second grade, is certainly prime time for guided reading. After all, you have just launched kids into reading small collections of books at their assessed levels. You'll also provide focused small-group instruction to support students' ability to transfer their knowledge of word study principles into reading. For example, you may gather a group of students who have been studying closed and open syllables during word work and say, "Readers—writers—let's set up our white boards to do some word work just like we do during word study time! We know that some vowels go together in words to make one sound, usually the sound of the name of the first vowel, though not always." This may be review work of phonics teaching that typically takes place with readers at levels G/H/I. After warm-up work with vowel teams, you can help students transfer this knowledge as they read a continuous text, working with flexibility, particularly on the middle parts of tricky words.

As this bend continues, you'll let students know that a word can be tricky even when they can *read* the word. You might say, "Readers understand that easy words aren't always as easy as they seem. Once readers figure out how to *say* a word, they know to stop and think, 'Wait, but what does this word mean in this story?'" To illustrate this point, we suggest you ask children to make a little sketch that shows what they think the word *fixing* means. Children will probably draw hammers and nails, which can lead you to ask students to read a sentence in which *fixing* relates to lunch, not carpentry, allowing you to make the point that some words have secondary meanings.

As you bring this bend to a close, you'll want to drive home the importance of quick word solving in reading. Tell your children the story of a botched joke. "I just got a new joke book," you might say. "I love joke books, and I *love* making my brother laugh, so I called him up last night to read him some of the jokes." Then, share the joke you messed up: "Question: How do you know when it's raining cats and dogs? Answer: When you step into a *puddle*!" When the class gives you that I-don't-get-it-face, you can admit, "Not that funny, right? You all reacted just like my brother did—except, then he added, 'Are you sure you read that right?' When I looked at the book again, I realized it said, 'Question: How do you know when it's raining cats and dogs? Answer: When you step into a *poodle*!'" This will be your opportunity to make the bigger point, "We all make mistakes, but if you catch them, quickly and *by yourself*, you can make your reading stronger." And so as this bend comes to a close, you will invite your students to seal their commitment to help themselves with a pledge: "I do solemnly promise to fix my *own* mistakes when I read."

Bend III: Paying Close Attention to Authors

In the final bend, you'll begin by helping readers use what they know as writers to help them grow as readers. You'll tell the kids about a time when you were invited backstage to meet one of the dancers in a ballet show. You pulled the curtain back to reveal *everything*! There were people and lights and pulleys and so many props. You got a glimpse of how the ballet was *made*, how every part was *crafted*. Readers, too, can pull back the curtain on the books they love, to think about how an author crafted the story! You'll show your readers how every time they react to their book, with a chuckle or a gasp or a wide-eyed stare, the author was hard at work writing a sentence or choosing a phrase that would make them *react*. Over the course of this bend, readers will look for this kind of powerful writing and ask, "How did the author do that?" and then "Why did the author do that?"

To launch this bend, you'll announce that starting today children will apply what they are learning as writers to their work as readers—they will learn to read like writers. You'll say, "Readers, have you noticed that you've been growing like beanstalks every day, not *just* as readers, but as *writers*, too? Well, guess what? You are now ready to take what you've learned in writing to grow your reading! It's almost like you can climb our beanstalk into writing workshop, collect all you've learned there, and bring it back down to reading workshop to help you read and think in new ways! But for this new growth to happen, you need to start reading like writers—not just when we read books during writing workshop—but when you read *any* book, *any* time."

Once children are noticing the craft in their independent reading books and analyzing the techniques authors use to build these crafted stories, you'll invite them to try those techniques in their own writing. In this session, you'll tell your students to set up for reading time with both reading *and* writing materials. Then you'll teach them that readers who are also *writers* don't just sit around admiring masterful writing. You'll say, "When readers notice an author's craft move—and they *really* love it—they take action. They try it in their *own* writing." Then in what will likely prove to be an extra-long workshop

period, you'll invite children to read a bit and then write a bit, trying out all the craft techniques they so admire.

As the bend continues, you will open the door to helping children see that the stories they read don't just appear, and that author's craft goes beyond the word of choosing the perfect word or writing a clever phrase. You'll point out that authors work long and hard to make *all* the parts of the story click together, especially the ending. You'll explain, "Authors work carefully to fit the parts of the story together, making all the parts connect and leaving the reader with an ending that ties it all up and often teaches an important lesson." This will lead in to the important work of teaching readers to make sense of the endings in their stories, helping them to see how each part of the story works with what comes before and after to build towards the ideas and lessons authors are trying to convey.

To celebrate the work of this unit, you'll rally children to reflect on all the ways they have grown in the few short weeks since school began. After cheers and congratulations have been passed from child to child, you might add, "So far this year, I've been teaching you all kinds of things to help you grow like beanstalks, and, my goodness, you certainly have grown! I'm thinking that today, instead of me teaching you something new, you could actually share what you know with other readers. You could help other readers grow! Are you up for it?"

Next you can invite them to find their very favorite books from the last few weeks and fill those books with important pieces of advice for future readers. Once your readers have written their words of wisdom on Post-its and left them on the covers of their books, you'll invite them to join you in a circle with all the books for a messy—and fun!—library reorganization party. You might say to kids, "You left such powerful tips for readers in your books today. I'm thinking that one more place you could give advice today is in our classroom library. I have a bunch of empty bins here, and I was thinking you might want to reorganize our books in some way." Maybe one bin could have books they especially recommend, and another bin could contain books that teach readers life lessons. And a third could have books with really tricky phrases. Eventually you could also invite kids to look at the books in their baggies and think about how they want to organize them. Perhaps some of them go together as books that illustrate the lessons, "Friends make a difference!" or "Don't give up!"

ASSESSMENT

In the first few days, observe your readers carefully. This will help you determine where to start your running records.

During the first few days of school, you'll want to invite readers into your classroom and set them at ease, allowing them to show off all that they already know. To do this, you can cluster them around tubs of books that approximate their reading levels from last year. That is, if you have readers who read level I at the end of last year, you'll seat them at a table with a tub of books that hold level H/I/J books. This will allow children access to books that are likely to be just right for them, plus it will allow you to see to how comfortable children are in those levels and at which levels you will likely start your running record assessments.

At this point in the year, many of your readers will be reading level I/J/K books to meet the end-of-the-year benchmark of level M. Many will make progress quickly, moving to level J/K/L by November and then to level K/L by January. Keep in mind that as the books children read increase in length, it often takes them a bit longer to move up in levels. You can expect that children who make this kind of quick progress in the first half of the year may be reading level L/M by March and end the year solidly reading the benchmark level M text.

Start your formal running records and move children into their just-right levels.

After the first days of watching over children's shoulders, chatting with them about their reading lives, and listening in on their conversations with one another, you can begin conducting running records. One way to do this efficiently is to sit at a table of like readers and move from child to child conducting your running records. If you need support in how to administer these, you can learn more about running records in Chapter 6 in *A Guide to the Reading Workshop, Primary Grades*. For now, it is important to remember that you get through these assessments quickly and that you try another, more challenging text after the child seems to be reading at his or her just-right level. You won't know if you have reached the maximum level unless you go beyond that point, assessing at a higher level.

Once you've administered running records, you will know what goals to set to move that reader forward and help her grow stronger and stronger. If a child seems almost at that next level, you might suggest she move into a mixed baggie at the beginning of Bend II, with some books that are easy and some that are the next level up (at the child's instructional level).

Look more closely at students who are not meeting the benchmark or students whose reading puzzles you.

You'll likely encounter children whom you are concerned about—students whose reading level is below the benchmark, or even students who are reading on benchmark but for whom you aren't sure what to focus on. When it isn't clear what to do next for a student, you want to do more assessments to get to the bottom of things. Running records alone might not tell you the whole picture, so you will also assess their knowledge of high-frequency words, conduct a spelling inventory, and assess their ability to match letters with sounds. With this information in hand, you can then develop a theory about the reader, and design instruction that closely matches the needs of each reader. Ideally, you can draw on the support of a school reading specialist or literacy coach to help administer these assessments and devise plans for each at-risk reader. Certainly, if a student is receiving additional help, you will want to be sure that help is coordinated with the help the child receives in your class. Chapter 6 in *A Guide to the Reading Workshop, Primary Grades* will provide more detail about where to find and how to administer these additional assessments.

Of course, you'll also begin conducting ongoing formative assessments: conferring one-to-one, holding table conferences with groups of kids, collecting reading logs, and planning next steps for your class. This less formal data can support you in making curricular decisions for reading workshop or even word study time.

GETTING READY

Use assessment data from the end of first grade to prepare your classroom library, and begin filling table-top tubs with books for students to share.

To begin the year, students will read from tubs of leveled high-interest fiction books. You'll fill these tubs with books that match the levels in the assessment data you have from students at the end of first grade. It would be terrific if you could borrow books from your first-grade colleagues—books that their first-graders enjoyed towards the end of first grade—so that your tubs can include familiar books that students can reread. Arrange students around the tub that matches their just-right level, based on the available data regarding students' reading levels from the end of first grade. For example, you might have a number of level G/H tubs, a level I/J/K tub, and if need be, a level E/F tub. Of course, you may also have readers who are outside of these ranges, and you'll need to identify these students early on so you can alter the book tubs to include leveled books below or above this range, or supply these children with individual leveled baggies as soon as possible.

Meanwhile, you'll also want to set up your classroom library organized by levels and genres. By the beginning of Bend II, you want to be ready for children to choose their own books guided by the leveled baskets you have created. As you collect running records and match students to current just-right levels, you'll set up a book shopping routine and transition all students into individual reading baggies for independent reading.

Collect texts you will use for minilessons, shared reading, and read-aloud, as well as guided reading.

Gather texts you will use for minilessons, shared reading, read-aloud, and small-group work using high-interest books that will reflect the reading your students will be doing. This unit suggests using texts such as *Katie Woo Has the Flu* by Fran Manushkin, as well as other popular series such as Fly Guy, Cam Jansen, Dragon, and Frog and Toad. The better you know these books, the better you will be able to use them to teach.

Gather other materials you'll use to support second-graders as you launch reading workshop routines, including bookmarks, reading logs, Post-its, and take-home book baggies.

You'll want to gather a few other important materials to support your second-grade readers as you launch this year's reading workshop. Since students are sharing tubs of books, make sure to have a few bookmarks handy so that students reading longer books can save their spot from day to day. This will also support them in rebuilding the habit of finishing a text before moving onto a new one. Distribute Post-its in each table tub, as they will be a necessity this year. Make sure you have plenty of Post-its ready to use as you teach, too. You'll also introduce reading logs as you teach children to begin to track their reading and build stamina and volume as readers. By Bend II, you'll move children out of the shared tubs of books and into independent baggies of books, and you may want to prepare take-home book baggies to

again support reading stamina and volume both at school and at home. These materials will be resources you'll want to have available for students to use all throughout the year.

Use charts from first grade to refresh readers and to review reading strategies and routines. Prepare the new charts to lift the level of these strategies and routines for second-graders.

You might launch this new year of reading workshop by displaying some of the reading charts from the end of the first grade. Your colleagues in first grade won't mind sharing these charts, as they will hopefully be doing the same thing—borrowing from kindergarten. We suggest displaying charts that review familiar strategies and routines so they are ready to refer to at the very beginning of the year. You'll, of course, want to have chart paper ready to make new second-grade strategy, stamina, and routine charts as well. Remember that the charts you'll want to use to support your students are provided throughout the unit. Finally, you'll establish a word wall that will grow and change throughout the year.

Consider how you will set up reading partnerships right from the start of the unit and again as you assess students and collect data.

In the beginning of the year, you'll want to partner up students so they can begin thinking and talking together right away. You might want to arrange students in the meeting area based on the data you have from the end of first grade, just as you arranged students around table tubs. As you assess, you'll collect data to help you establish reading partnerships by considering students' interests, current reading levels, strengths and skills. You'll want to have these partnerships established by the second bend of the unit.

Use the read-aloud plan at the back of this book to prepare for one read-aloud across a couple of days, as well as others across the unit.

Read-aloud is an important part of instruction in a balanced literacy framework. First and foremost, there is no better way to build a community of readers than to share engaging texts that spark lively discussions and open dialogue. Children will get to know each other as they discuss the characters and information in the texts you share with them. During read-aloud, you'll want to read books at levels at or slightly above end of year benchmarks (approximately levels M/N/O). Engaging with high-level complex texts gives students the opportunity to analyze texts they may not yet be able to access independently. This sets students up to think deeply and to practice comprehension skills and strategies with the support of the class as a whole—skills they will need to utilize independently by year's end.

Select books that are engaging, complex stories that will be fun to talk and think about.

Those Darn Squirrels was chosen as the first picture book read-aloud. This book has many elements that make it a great choice for the start of second grade. First, it is a very funny book. Humor is a major component of the books second-graders will be reading and much of the difficulty that second-graders encounter involves understanding what makes their books funny. *Those Darn Squirrels* is a quirky story full of humor that demands the children think deeply too. And though the book does have a problem and a solution, the solution is not the most expected outcome. Instead of Fookwire getting what he *thinks* he wants, he gets something else. These challenges in the text push children to think carefully about the various elements of the story in order to understand the bigger ideas. The message of finding friendship in unusual places is perfect for the beginning of the year as children begin to form their own new friendships.

The read-aloud plan at the back of this book will help you to support student thinking. You will find prompts that help you engage your students in taking a meaningful sneak peek of the book; predicting, confirming, and revising during your first reading of the text; and retelling this more complex story. In your second reading, you are encouraged to dig deeper with your students, helping them to find ways in which the story fits together. You'll help students notice the author's craft as the author makes each part of the story fit with what came before. Then, too, you'll help children to find the lessons the author illustrates in the book. You will also see that in your packet you have yellow Post-it notes, with the prompts written on them, which you can place directly into your own copy of the book. You will then be able to take out these Post-it notes and use them in another read-aloud text that you select. All of the prompts are transferable across texts.

Consider other types of texts you may want to read aloud.

Picture books are important for second-grade readers, because they often contain complex plots, crafted writing, and messages that speak directly to readers' lives. In addition to modern stories, you are encouraged to read fairy tales throughout the school year. Exposing children to both the traditional and fractured tales will help them to develop story sense and an understanding of character types—the wise one, the trickster, the fool—that will populate the books they will read for years to come.

You'll also want to read chapter books with your class right from the start. We suggest books that could be an introduction to a series that children will soon read on their own. One such book is *Mercy Watson to the Rescue*. This text is a little closer to the children's independent level, which leaves you the opportunity to read it to your children and then choose a chapter to study in shared reading as well.

Use the five-day plan in the back of this book to help you prepare for shared reading.

After the read-aloud template in the back of the book you will find a five-day plan for shared reading. We suggest that after you read and discuss the book *Mercy Watson to the Rescue* during read-aloud time, you select Chapter 3 to study closely in shared reading. We have selected this book for many reasons. First, this book is a level K early chapter book, and many of your students will be reading these types of books at the beginning of the year. Shared reading will be the perfect setting to immerse children in the reading behaviors required for this kind of book. Second, like *Those Darn Squirrels*, *Mercy Watson to the Rescue* employs humor as a way to engage and challenge readers through its use of idioms and homophones. You'll find yourself checking in to make sure that your students truly understand all the nuances and clever jokes.

Shared reading provides opportunities to practice the main skills your readers will learn in this unit of study.

You will find a five-day plan for shared reading in the back of this book. Each day will have a warm-up, a focused reading, and an after-reading extension. Though your shared reading sessions will last only fifteen minutes, you'll find that your students will gain skills and strategies quickly as they study the text across days. In your first shared reading of the text, you'll work with children to read with accuracy, fixing mistakes as they read, and to retell the story in meaningful chunks. In your second reading, you'll help children focus on word solving, studying and checking their reading to make sure it looks right, sounds right, and makes sense. During the third reading, you'll call closer attention to word work, even removing words from the text to study their spelling patterns. On day four, you will help children read with fluency—an important skill as the sentences in their texts become longer and harder to read with appropriate phrasing. Finally, your fifth reading can focus on higher-level comprehension. Here you can facilitate a conversation in which the children think about how this chapter of text fits with what happens before and after it.

✸ ONLINE DIGITAL RESOURCES

A variety of resources to accompany this and the other Grade 2 Units of Study for Teaching Reading are available in the Online Resources, including charts and examples of student work shown throughout *Second-Grade Reading Growth Spurt*, as well as links to other electronic resources. Offering daily support for your teaching, these materials will help you provide a structured learning environment that fosters independence and self-direction.

To access and download all the digital resources for the Grade 2 Units of Study for Teaching Reading:

1. Go to **www.heinemann.com** and click the link in the upper right to log in. (If you do not have an account yet, you will need to create one.)
2. **Enter the following registration code** in the box to register your product: RUOS_Gr2
3. Under **My Online Resources**, click the link for the *Grade 2 Reading Units of Study*.
4. The digital resources are available in the upper right; click a file name to download. (For any compressed ("ZIP") files, double-click the downloaded file to extract individual files to your hard drive.)

(You may keep copies of these resources on up to six of your own computers or devices. By downloading the files you acknowledge that they are for your individual or classroom use and that neither the resources nor the product code will be distributed or shared.)

Readers Choose *How* to Read

IN THIS SESSION, you'll teach children that as readers grow, they get to choose not only *what* they are going to read but also *how* they are going to read.

GETTING READY

✔ Place bins of books at the center of each table before this session begins. Use a list of last year's reading levels to seat children around a bin that contains books those children are apt to be able to read. Add a pack of Post-it® notes to each bin and keep one handy to use yourself.

✔ Use the start of the nursery rhyme, book, or song, *There Was an Old Lady Who Swallowed a Fly* (see Teaching and Active Engagement).

✔ Help children partner up to read *There Was an Old Lady Who Swallowed a Fly* together. Consider keeping the partnerships until Bend 2, when assessment-based partnerships are established (see Active Engagement).

✔ Gather two books of different levels to demonstrate children's growth in reading (see Link).

✔ Prepare a chart titled "Readers GROW Like Beanstalks!" and make sure the strategy "Decide HOW to read" is ready to add to the chart (see Link).

✔ During reading workshop, plan to seat kids around bins of books that reflect last year's reading level (see Conferring and Small-Group Work).

✔ Place bookmarks in book bins (see Share).

✔ Make sure the "Reading Partners Work Together" chart from first grade is ready to refer to (see Share).

MINILESSON

CONNECTION

Glory in the newfound growth of your second-graders. They're taller, and they have big-kid privileges and responsibilities. Use this drumroll to suggest they'll want to grow as readers, too.

"Second-graders, you are all becoming so grown up! So many changes! How many of you got taller this summer?" Lots of children signaled yes, and I called on a few to stand up and show us.

"Growing up means you get to do more cool stuff, right? Are any of you getting new bedtimes? Getting to watch new shows? Yes? Wait, wait, I have a better question. Are any of you getting new chores? Turn and tell the person beside you how things are changing for you because you are older."

❖ **Name the teaching point.**

"Readers, today I want to teach you that reading, also, changes as you get older. Second-grade readers don't only get to read harder and longer books; they also get to be in charge of their own reading. They get to choose not only *what* they are going to read but also *how* they are going to read."

TEACHING

Explain that now, as second-graders, they can choose how they'll read a book. Show how to do this by reading a familiar song or story in a manner most children wouldn't have chosen for that text.

"Little kids just pick up a book and—read it. But as second-graders, you know that you don't just read a book; first you think, '*How* will I read this?' You think, 'Do I want to read this in a funny, singsongy way? Do I want to read it slowly, thinking really deeply about each page before moving on? Do I want to read this like it is an exciting story, and try to feel the excitement of it?

"Let's try that together," I said, and held up the book *There Was an Old Lady Who Swallowed a Fly*.

"Hmm, . . . how do I want to read *this* book?" I mused. "Well, she dies, so I'll read it in a very serious, sad way. I'll use my voice to sound sad and serious," I said, jotting the words *serious* and *sad* on a big Post-it note and placing it on the cover of the book. Then, I started reading the text with a very solemn expression, giving great weight to each word.

> There was an old lady who swallowed a fly. I don't know why she
>
> Swallowed that fly.
>
> Perhaps she'll die.

Debrief, highlighting the transferability of what you just did.

"Did you see that like all of you, I took charge of my reading? I decided not just *what* to read, but also *how* to read. I read that song like it is a sad, sad story. It's *my* reading, and I could have read it differently."

ACTIVE ENGAGEMENT

Highlight that as second-graders, children can choose not only *what* but also *how* they'll read a text. Then channel them to make a choice and to read with partners as chosen.

"The good news is that because you, as second-graders, are in charge of your reading, you get to decide *how* you will read something, and you can decide to read the same text more than one time—reading it differently each time. Right now, will you think how *you* would like to read this same book. Do you want to read it in a songlike way?" I sang just three words to prime the pump of that option. "Or do you want to read this like it is a creepy, scary story, meant to give people the shivers? Or do you want to read this like you are a news reporter, making an announcement about this old lady on 96th Street," I spoke in my best newscaster voice, "who swallowed a fly.

"Right now, find a person near you to work with. Together, pick a way to read this text, and then get started reading it however the two of you decide. You can read in unison or take turns. Go!"

For now, don't explain that some ways of reading the book are more appropriate for the text. Don't work hard to explain your rationale. And know that we are deliberately suggesting you read the text in a manner the children won't be apt to choose, because you are leaving the easier option for them to use during the active engagement section.

As silly as this sounds, your reference to little kids needs to be made as if your kids are not little kids anymore. You are saying, "Long, long ago, when you were little, you just picked up a book and read it, but now, as a great big second-grader, you know better."

You may wonder why it is so important that kids get to choose how they will read a text—and you are right to question whether this is worth highlighting. But here's the thing: you are subtly informing kids that they read with a sense of agency. You are also supporting the fact that kids reread texts often. Then, too, you are suggesting that readers set goals and choose lenses. So we think there is enough about this instruction to make it worth doing.

Recruit a few volunteers to read just a tiny bit of the text aloud, illustrating the many options (and the fun of reading).

One set of partners read a few lines in spooky voices before I cut them off to showcase, next, some *American Idol* wannabes.

I summarized, "It's fun, isn't it, to choose *how* you want to read a book, and to realize you can read the same book in different ways."

LINK

Revisit the theme that second grade is a year for enormous growth. Like the magic beans in "Jack and the Beanstalk," readers will grow and grow this year. To get started, they choose not only *what* but also *how* to read.

"At the start of today's minilesson, you told me that because you are in second grade now, some of you have new bed-times, new jobs, new privileges. And I hope you are learning that reading, too, changes when you get to be in second grade. In this one school year, you are going to change from reading books like this," and I opened a level H book, "to reading books like this." I opened a very popular level N book. "In the whole of your life, you will probably never grow as fast as you are going to grow this year.

"Do some of you remember, in the story 'Jack and the Beanstalk,' how Jack traded his cow for some magic beans, and his mother threw those beans out the window? But that night, the beans grew into a beanstalk, and the beanstalk grew and grew and *grew* so that Jack, in the morning, was able to climb up to the magic kingdom, where he found the hen that laid golden eggs.

"I'm reminding you about that story because you should know that there are scientists, researchers, who study young kids as readers, and they say that in this one year, you are going to grow and grow and *grow* just like that beanstalk! To do that growing, you need to start *today*. You get to choose not just *what* you will read, but also *how* you will read." I uncovered the anchor chart.

Send kids off to start reading at their tables. Make this transition quick so as to use every bit of reading time.

"So head off, lickety-split, to your tables. Let's not waste even a minute, going one table at a time. You'll find a bin of books at your table. Take a book, decide how to read it, and write your decision on a Post-it, and then read the book. Remember, even when you are reading in your *head*, you can make your reading voice change. After you read one way, choose a different way, and read that same book again in that different way. You game? Off you go!"

The idea of this unit centers on the reading growth spurt that children will experience this year, so dramatizing how different these two books look and feel is important. You want your students to gasp when they realize that the end-of-the-year level looks so very grown-up and exciting.

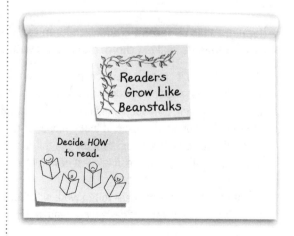

First Day Settling and Connecting

APPROACH TODAY'S WORKSHOP knowing that you have only today and part of tomorrow to help each child feel seen and respected within your reading workshop, because then you will need to devote the lion's share of each workshop to getting your assessments done. So today, make a special point to create moments of closeness around reading with each child.

Before you can do that, however, you'll need to spin around the room and settle kids into the work of the day. We recommend using last year's reading levels to cluster small groups of students who are apt to read at a similar level around the same bin of books. Once kids are reading from bins that contain books at a few consecutive levels, you can quickly scan the class and, within just a few minutes, get a sense of who is engrossed in their books and who may be holding books that are too hard. This, then, will allow you to check your first hunches about text levels. It will also make it easier for you (a few days from now) to give running records to a small group of similar readers.

It will help to imagine the challenges you'll encounter and to anticipate your responses. Some children may be standing above their bins, stirring the books about or sifting through the collection; these children will need help committing to a single book and settling down to read it. If this is the case for many kids in the classroom, rely on a voiceover to channel the whole class toward settling down. "I'm seeing that by now, most of you have chosen a book you can actually read, a book you can spend some time with, and you are deep into reading the start of that book. Nice work. If you haven't selected one book to read, starting at the front and reading every page, do so now."

Other children may be making it hard for classmates to read—perhaps out of enthusiasm. You'll want to protect that enthusiasm, doing the necessary classroom management work while still championing the joy of reading. "Sarah, can you see that Jose is *dying* to read his book? I know you are excited to share your book, but save the sharing for later." "John, I just know you don't want to miss another precious moment of reading time! Get started—right away, my friend!"

Then, once the class is settled, move among readers, listening, talking with great interest about the books and the different ways the children are reading them—talking with children as you would talk with a colleague about books. Say things like, "Oh my goodness, this book is *so* beautifully written. Don't you just love the sound of the words?" And then read a bit. Or "I've been watching how focused you are on reading. You're the kind of reader who opens a book and gets lost in the story, aren't you?"

As you touch base with readers, be extremely perceptive of any signs that readers are matched with appropriately leveled texts, because you will very soon need to start conducting running records, and to do so you will want to be able to estimate the approximate level of difficulty that each child can handle.

MID-WORKSHOP TEACHING
Reading Slowly and Thoughtfully

"Readers, I'm noticing that many of you are reading books quickly—almost like you think reading quickly is the best way to read. And it is true that when you are just starting to read, instead of reading, 'I. See. The. Dog,' readers put words together, reading faster: 'I see the dog.' But, as you get to be a *second-grade* reader, you don't keep going faster and faster: 'Iseethedog.' Second-grade readers know the best thing is to sometimes read fast and smooth ('I see the dog.') and to sometimes read slowly and thoughtfully. ('I see . . . the dog . . . Whoa! Look at his curly hair!') The reason to read a book slowly is that you can notice more and think more. ('Look at that fur. Why is it so matted?') So, readers, make sure that some of the time, you are choosing to read *thoughtfully*."

Reviewing Partner Reading

Demonstrating what they know from prior years, partners practice reading together by sitting hip to hip, holding a shared book, and talking about how they'll read before starting to do so.

"Readers, please find a good place to stop your reading. If you are in the middle of a book, put your bookmark at your page." I motioned to the bookmarks that I had placed in the book bins. "When you are ready, put all your books back in the bin, except for the book you are in the midst of reading. Bring that book with you and join me in the meeting area."

Once they'd settled, I said, "For your share time today, and usually, you'll do partner reading. Right now, without anyone saying anything, will you show me what you already know about how to read with a partner? Quick as wink, show me what you do during partner reading."

I watched as most kids sat hip to hip, fumbling between their two books. "I love that you are sitting hip to hip because that's a great way to share books. But some of you aren't actually *sharing* books. Do this. Start with one partner. That partner gets to choose a book for you two to read together. Put the book between the two of you, with both of you holding one side of the book. Do that now."

The kids held their books in position. "Now, tell me—do you just open the book and start reading?" Without waiting for responses, I answered my question. "No way! Instead, you talk about *how* you'll read the book." I gestured to a partner reading chart from first grade. "How many of you remember this chart?" Most children did, so I signaled them to use the chart to help them talk through alternative ways of reading, and then to get started.

ANCHOR CHART

Reading Partners Work Together

- We work as a team. (sit side by side, book in the middle, take turns)
- We build good habits together. (sneak peeks, do things at the end of books, reread books)
- We read together. (choral read, echo read, seesaw read)
- We give reminders. ("Don't forget to . . ." "Try this instead . . .")
- We grow ideas together. ("I never thought about that!")
- We give book introductions.
- We don't just tell—we HELP!
- We do SOMETHING at the end. (reread, smooth it out, retell, share ideas)

Second-Grade Readers Take a Sneak Peek to Decide How a Book *Wants* to Be Read

MINILESSON

CONNECTION

Celebrate the good start you saw yesterday, noting that children were not only choosing *what* to read but also *how*.

After children settled into the meeting area, each carrying a book, I said, "When I was your age, my parents stuck a measuring tape giraffe onto one of our walls, and my brothers and sisters and I stood against it, heels to the wall, head up, so my parents could mark our height and check how much we'd grown. I wish we had taken your height as readers yesterday because I am pretty sure that you are *already* growing.

"I know that at school yesterday and at home last night, many of you didn't just read; you chose *how* you were going to read. What are some ways that you read?"

Child after child chimed in: some read quickly; some read slowly; some read in a songlike way; some did silly, scary, or thoughtful readings. I nodded, adding, "And you didn't read books just once, did you? How many of you did some rereading yesterday?" Hands shot up around the room.

❖ **Name the teaching point.**

"Today I want to teach you that when readers choose how they are going to read a book, it helps them to think, 'How does this book *want* to be read?' To answer that, readers give the book a sneak peek—a grown-up, second-grade sneak peek."

IN THIS SESSION, you'll teach children that before reading, it helps readers to look the book over, using a sneak peek to decide how the book *wants* be read.

GETTING READY

✔ Ask students to select from the table bin a just-right book that they have not yet read and bring it to the meeting area (see Connection).

✔ Display the anchor chart you started in Session 1, "Readers GROW Like Beanstalks!" on the easel and make sure the strategy "Give the book a sneak peek" is ready to add to the chart (see Connection).

✔ Choose a demonstration text that you'll carry across the bend. *Katie Woo Has the Flu*, by Fran Manushkin, illustrated by Tammie Lyon, is a good choice because it is a text that features an engaging plotline and a memorable character and is at the benchmark level for the beginning of second grade. Enlarge the cover, back of the book, and the table of contents, or display them on a document camera (see Teaching).

✔ Designate a Partner 1 and Partner 2 in each partnership (see Active Engagement).

✔ Plan to seat kids during the reading workshop around bins of books that you believe are probably within grasp for those kids (see Link).

✔ During reading workshop, plan to seat kids around bins of books that you believe are probably within grasp. This may mean rearranging a few children from Session 1's seating to reflect what you observe now (see Conferring and Small-Group Work).

✔ Prepare to assess as many children as you can by using running records (see Conferring and Small-Group Work).

✔ Be ready to distribute Post-its to partnerships (see Share).

I added the new strategy to the anchor chart.

TEACHING

Point out that the song you read aloud so somberly the day before was written as a silly song, and use that point to advocate for readers taking a sneak peek to decide how to read a book.

"Yesterday I decided to read *There Was an Old Lady Who Swallowed a Fly* as a very serious story of a poor old woman who died. But here's the problem. Texts are written so they almost *want* to be read in particular ways. And although I *could* read *There Was an Old Lady Who Swallowed a Fly* as a sad, serious story, it's written as a *silly* song, to be sung happily!" To illustrate, the kids and I sang just a bit of the song.

"So today, I want to point out that even before you start reading a book, it helps to look the book over, using a sneak peek to decide how the book *wants* to be read.

"Together, let's do a grown-up, second-grade sneak peek with *Katie Woo Has the Flu*." I held up the book and said, "We'll still look at—really, study—the cover, right?" and I showed it to the class. Nodding as if confirming what they were thinking, I said, "So this gives us the idea to read the book in a serious, worried way because she's sick." The children nodded, but I didn't wait for full responses. "In second grade, is that *all* you do to get ready to read? No!" I turned to the back of the book, looking out at the class as I tapped the back blurb. "I'll read it, and let's think together about whether this helps us think how the book *wants* to be read. Is this going to be super sad or what?" I read the back cover:

> Hi! I'm Katie Woo.
> My mom says that I have a bug.
> I thought that meant there is a
> bug running around in my tummy.
> But it just means I am sick. Now
> I have to stay home from school
> and eat boring things like soup

Readers GROW Like Beanstalks!

- Decide HOW to read.
- **Give the book a sneak peek.**

Encouraging the work children did on Day One is key, but don't take too long to do this. Calling on one child at a time often draws out this sharing for too long. Instead, set the stage so that children learn to call out their answers one after another, without pause. Learning to do this respectfully will be part of the growth you seek in your second-graders.

Reading the back blurb and the table of contents will be an important next step if most of your children are reading at benchmark. If the majority of your students are reading at level G and below, you will want to adjust this lesson to review the first-grade sneak peek, putting emphasis instead on studying the cover, peeking at a few pages, and thinking about what might happen in the story.

and toast. Why won't this flu bug
just go away?

"Hmm, . . . so what hints does this give us about how the book *wants* to be read? I'm starting to wonder if it's not really serious and worried at all. It seems like Katie is confused about being sick because it says she thinks there is a bug in her tummy. It also says that she can't go to school and she has to eat boring soup, so maybe it wants to be read with a boring, annoyed voice. What are you thinking?" Children called out ideas as I flipped to the table of contents.

"Readers, now that this is second grade, you can do even more in our sneak peek. You can also look at the table of contents and ask yourselves," I gestured for the class to chime in, "'How does this book *want* to be read?' Let's read it together."

> *Chapter 1: Ah-choo!*
>
> *Chapter 2: Sick at Home*
>
> *Chapter 3: Feeling Better*

"Hmm, . . . it sounds like Katie gets sick in the first chapter. Maybe that's when she is confused about the bug in her tummy. Maybe that part will want to be read in a confused voice." I read the title, "Ah-choo!" in a confused voice, shrugging my shoulders and furrowing my brows.

"In Chapter 2, she stays home from school. I wonder if she's bored because she's home in bed all day. I bet that chapter will be read in a bored voice." I reread the chapter title, this time in a bored, monotonous voice.

"Then at the end, it seems she feels better. Hmm, . . . maybe that part wants to be read in a relieved, happier voice." I read the last chapter title with a distinct change in my voice, reading with a peppy upbeat voice to match how this part of the book might want to be read.

Debrief, naming the things you did to orient yourself to a book that you hope others do as well.

"Second-graders, when you did sneak peeks in first grade, you looked at the cover and peeked at a few pages. Am I right? Now, as second-graders, you will do even more during your sneak peeks—reading the blurb and the table of contents—so that you can think about not only what the book might be about but also how your book or parts of your book want to be read."

Here you will want to model the real reading work involved in studying the table of contents. While children might just read the words, be sure you stop to discuss what might happen in each chapter. This sets readers up to synthesize text later.

ACTIVE ENGAGEMENT

Invite students to choose how they want to get ready to read.

"Right now, Partner 1, take out the book you brought with you to the meeting area. Before you decide *how* you want to read it, take a sec' to think, 'How does this book *want* to be read?' To figure that out, work with Partner 2 to give it a sneak peek—a *second-grade* sneak peek." As the kids worked, I coached with some voiceovers:

"Don't forget to flip to the back to check if there's a blurb."

"Peek inside, at the table of contents."

"Help your partner think about how the book *wants* to be read!"

"Try reading the first little bit. That will give you an idea for how the book wants to be read, too."

After a minute, I said, "You already know quite a lot about the book you are about to read. So now, remember—you are in charge of your reading. You get to decide not only what you are going to read but also how you will read it. Tell each other how you think the book *wants* to be read, and then get started reading it that way!"

The room filled with voices as kids began reading their books aloud to each other. I didn't wait for them to read much before pressing on.

You will want to match your coaching to the levels of text children are holding. For students reading levels F/G, you might coach them to spend more time thinking about what the title reveals. For students reading levels L/M, you might suggest that different chapters will likely want to be read differently.

LINK

Suggest that readers are in charge of their own reading lives. Ask children to preview books and remind them that they have choices for *how* to read, too.

"Second-graders, you'll again be reading from a bin of books at the center of your table. Remember that you are in charge of your reading—and that means choosing what you'll read, as well as choosing how you'll read it. So before you do anything else, take some time to choose a book that is just right for you. Then, do a sneak peek, thinking, 'How does this book *want* to be read?' And remember, books can be read many times, many ways, and you can read a book more than once."

FIG. 2–1 Bookmarks with students' names help readers find their book (and the page where they left off) when reading from a shared bin of books.

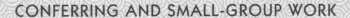

Starting Running Records while Managing a Classroom of Readers

B Y THE END OF THIS BEND, you'll need to have assessed your readers so that you can put them into matched partnerships, so that means you will need to begin conducting running records today. Start by spending time getting an approximate sense of the levels of text difficulty that kids can handle. Keep your clipboard at hand and note the level of book that each reader is reading and how well that reader can handle that book. Feel free to push readers a bit. If you want to test whether a reader can read a few notches higher than he is currently reading, say, "Can I interrupt you? While I'm here, I wonder if I could convince you to read this other book to me for just a minute. It's a book I really like, and I think you might like it too." We describe the process of giving running records in future Conferring and Small-Group Work sections and in *A Guide to the Reading Workshop, Primary Grades*.

Of course, it is still a priority for you to champion reading, to help children love reading. Even if your memory of some of the books children are reading is hazy, let readers know you love the book and the author. "Can I take a little turn reading this? It is one of my favorites," you can say, and then read a page or two to the child, exclaiming, "I wish *I* could take this book home. You are so lucky to have gotten to it first!" or "You are great at choosing good books to read, aren't you? This one has everything I love in it!" It is incredibly powerful to show that you love the book a child is reading.

You will also need to do some work to support a well-managed reading workshop. Children will probably come to you for many silly reasons. Instead of answering their questions and supporting their dependency, act surprised that they weren't able to figure things out for themselves, and do all you can to support independence. Only if kids can carry on without you will you be free to teach.

MID-WORKSHOP TEACHING

Readers Change How They Read, as They Read

Standing in the middle of the room, I voiced over, saying, "Readers, can I stop you for a moment? Some of you are realizing that your book has different parts, and each part has a different mood, a different feeling. So you are changing your voice as you read! Wow, that's really important work! Keep thinking and keep asking, 'How does *this* part want to be read?'"

Responding to How a Book *Wants* to Be Read

Channel kids to share in their own partnership places, first talking about how the shared book wants to be read, using Post-its to note variations in mood, and then reading aloud to each other.

I stood in the middle of the room and asked children to give me their attention. "Readers, we won't come together for a share session on the rug today. Instead, you and your partner will find your own places to share. In a minute, will you and your partner go to a sharing place and start talking about how one of your books wants to be read? Talk about whether the mood, the feeling, of the book changes so you and your partner should read with one voice early on and another later. If you decide that different parts of the book want to be read differently, you might want to leave little Post-its to yourself or to anyone else who comes to read this book, signaling how you think the book should be read. Then read aloud together—to each other or through your own shared reading.

"Go ahead and get to your sharing places and get started!"

Invite partnerships to read aloud to each other in ways that show how a page wants to be read.

"Readers, it's not fair that I'm the only one to hear the reading you and your partner are doing. We need to stage some performances! Quickly, pair up with another partnership or two, and find a space where you can perform for each other. Then will one reader (or one partnership) agree to go first? Read a few pages, using your voice to show the mood, or feeling, of the story—as you've been doing. Then another reader (or another partnership) can have a go.

"One tip. Be a little dramatic. If the passage is funny, ham it up, read in a way that gets your listeners laughing. If you are reading a scary part, read in ways that give your listeners goose bumps. Okay, get started!"

FIG. 2–2   Alice and Jackie use feeling Post-its to signal mood changes in their books.

Readers Get Stronger by Reading a Lot!

MINILESSON

IN THIS SESSION, you'll teach students that second grade can be a year when readers take off! And to do that, volume is key.

CONNECTION

Remind readers that earlier you compared second-grade reading growth to the growth of Jack's beanstalk, and ask, "How do readers get stronger?"

"Earlier, I told you that reading scientists have figured out that second grade is a time when readers shoot up, growing as if they were Jack's beanstalk. Remember how that beanstalk grew overnight until it reached the clouds? You won't grow *that* fast, but second grade *is* a really important year for readers to grow.

"But the thing is, you don't grow *taller* as readers. Instead, you grow stronger. And how do you think readers get stronger? Do readers lift weights? No! Do readers take vitamins? No!"

❖ **Name the teaching point.**

"Today I want to teach you that second-grade readers work hard to get stronger and stronger. To get stronger, they set goals, pushing themselves to read more and longer each day."

GETTING READY

✔ Spotlight one Fly Guy book, one Frog and Toad book, and one Cam Jansen book, or, if your children aren't familiar with these, three equivalently leveled books they do know, plus a Dragon book and a Katie Woo book (see Teaching).

✔ Display the anchor chart "Readers GROW Like Beanstalks!" on the easel and make sure the strategy "Read more and MORE!" is ready to add to the chart (see Teaching).

✔ Continue to use running records to assess children (see Conferring and Small-Group Work).

✔ Make a copy of the reading log for each student plus one to display (see Mid-Workshop Teaching).

✔ Prepare a stamina chart titled "Readers Read More and MORE! Growing Stamina Every Day" (see Share).

TEACHING

Tell students that reading researchers have found that when a child is matched to a book like the Fly Guy books, it should take five or ten minutes to read, and then talk up goal setting.

"Readers, eyes up here. I've been telling you about how there are scientists who study kids as readers. What you need to know is this: the scientists who have studied second-grade readers have made some announcements that are important for getting stronger as readers. They said that a book like the Fly Guy books should take you just five or so minutes to read! And that goes for all the books in the I basket." Holding up a Frog and Toad book, I said, "And a book like this, or any of the books from the J or K basket, should just take about ten minutes." Finally, I held up a Cam Jansen mystery. "Books like these, ones from the L or M basket, should take around forty-five minutes.

"They also said that it is a good thing for readers to set goals for themselves. So if this book," I held up a Fly Guy book "takes five minutes, I'm thinking that during our twenty-five minute reading time today, I should be able to read— wow!—*five* Fly Guy books.

"Of course, as second-graders, you don't read just those three books—instead, you read a lot of books that are sort of like one of those books. For example, I am not actually reading a Fly Guy book, but watch how I think about this." I picked up the book I was reading, looked at it, and said, "This Dragon book is about the same as a Fly Guy book, so that means I should be able to read five books like this during one day's reading time."

Debrief in ways that highlight the importance of readers working to get stronger. Suggest that one way to do this is to set goals for volume of reading.

"Did you see that to figure out a good goal for myself, a goal that could get me to push my reading muscles, I remembered that the reading scientists say that kids who can read Fly Guy books can read five of them in twenty-five minutes? A Katie Woo book seems about like a Fly Guy book, and they are both from the I basket, so I'm thinking that I should be able to read five Katie Woo books in twenty-five minutes, too!" After stacking up five books, I said, "Did you see how I figured out a *goal* for my reading time?"

Refer to the anchor chart, adding the latest strategy.

It is all too easy to throw a zillion little tips about reading at your kids, each disconnected from the next. If you hope to make an impact on your kids, if you want your teaching to be memorable, one day's teaching needs to fit, tongue and groove, into the next day's teaching, and you need to hearken back often to points made earlier. Notice that we do this here.

Of course, you hope that your students can sustain reading for twenty-five minutes right from the start, but this will not always be the case. If you have noticed that reading stamina in your class is very low, time your students to see how long they can stay focused during reading and then use the many tips in this session to grow their stamina.

If your children aren't familiar with Fly Guy, Frog and Toad, or Cam Jansen books, swap in other books they do know that are roughly equivalent, ones that match these in level. The point is that you have three books that represent the range of levels at which your children are reading.

ANCHOR CHART

Readers GROW Like Beanstalks!

- Decide HOW to read.
- Give the book a sneak peek.
- **Read more and MORE!**

ACTIVE ENGAGEMENT

Channel readers to calculate goals they can set, applying your figures to their own reading.

"Readers, take out your books, so you can set some goals too. Start by thinking about which kind of books you are reading. Are they mostly like Fly Guy books? Are they more like Cam Jansen books? How many books do you think you can read in one day's reading workshop? Think about it for a moment."

After kids thought silently, I said, "Whisper your goal to your partner. How many books will you read today? Partners, check to see if you think that it is a reasonable goal—not too much or too little. Remember, researchers say that if you are reading books like these," and I showed a few, "you should be able to read five of these in one workshop. If you are reading a book like this," and I showed a longer book, "you should be able to read one of these each day."

LINK

Send readers off to work with resolve.

"Readers, remember that today, our class goal is to read for not just twenty minutes, but for twenty-five minutes. Remember, you are the boss of your reading. You can decide not just *how* to read, but also, *how much* to read. To get stronger as a reader, set a goal. How many books will you read today? Then, work toward that goal. Off you go!"

Don't worry if your students are having trouble with the math here. Just ask them what they are reading and then help them come up with a goal.

Conducting Running Records Efficiently

BECAUSE YOU WILL NEED to devote most of your attention to assessing your readers, you'll need to rely on voiceovers to keep the whole class going. Your voiceovers will probably support kids' engagement in a volume of reading: "Push yourself to read more!" "When you finish one book, move to the next!"

Meanwhile, try to make your assessments efficient. For example, you will save huge amounts of time if you assess a cluster of similar readers at a time, instead of working in a one-to-one fashion. If your children have been sitting in temporary clusters based on the previous year's reading levels and you've already been getting a sense of which of the youngsters sitting around (say) the G bin of books can read those books easily and which are struggling a bit, you'll be in especially good shape to convene readers who seem able to handle roughly the same levels of text complexity. But even if you do this by relying only on the previous year's reading levels, you'll want to ask from three to five readers to gather around you and then explain to them what you'll be doing with them. Say, "I'll read with one of you, then the next. While I read with the others, you can turn like this," and show them how to turn their bodies away from you, "and read your own books to yourself. When I come to you, I'll ask you to read some particular books with me."

Once the group has all gotten started reading the first of a small pile of books to themselves, you can begin with the first reader, asking her to read aloud a benchmark text that you have chosen because you believe it will be a bit easy for each of the readers in this cluster. As that first reader reads the first one hundred words of the text, you mark the miscues and self-corrections and note fluency on the running record. Then direct her to continue reading the rest to herself while you turn to the next student and do the same thing with that student. Then while the second student reads silently, you can return to the first to ask comprehension questions. Such an arrangement not only saves time but also allows you to gauge students' work with a text in relation to others, which often provides further insight into strengths and needs.

When choosing the text level to use for the first assessment, err on the side of a text being too easy rather than too hard, so as not to deflate students' confidence and engagement. You'll want to be sure that when a child does read with 96% accuracy or higher (with satisfactory comprehension), you refrain from thinking "Bingo!" and

(continues)

MID-WORKSHOP TEACHING
Setting Goals for Volume and Stamina

"You have been reading for ten minutes straight, and you seem deep into it. In fact, I know that last year you used a reading log with tallies to keep track of how much you read. It seems like a log would help you right now, wouldn't it? I've made a new one that works better for readers like you, readers who are reading longer books, for longer amounts of time. I'm going to hand you these new logs and put a sample up on our document camera. Will you quickly start to fill them out with today's reading? If you have questions about the log, ask a neighbor. See if you can answer them together! Take out a Post-it, too. Jot your goal for today, so you can compare your goal with your log. Oh, and if you have already met your goal, set a new one."

Then a bit farther into reading time, the class became restless, so I spoke in a voiceover. "Readers, show me your muscles! Tell your partner how much you have read so far!" The room buzzed, and then, reconvening their attention, I said, "Are you game for reading more? Some of you may pass your goal—in which case, set a new goal! Let's try to read for another ten minutes. I think in that time, *everyone* can get to their goal! And we can set a new record for reading! Go!"

declaring that to be the child's level. He might do similar work at the next higher level, for all you know. Then, too, you need to conduct a running record at text levels that are high enough that the child makes enough miscues for you to analyze error patterns and notice how a reader responds in the face of difficulty. It's only when the child works just past her independent text level that you can discern what holds the reader back. Is this a reader who, when things start falling apart, holds on to meaning at all costs, generating words that may be incorrect but that nonetheless make sense, or is this a reader who relies so much on visual cues that she sacrifices the idea that readers construct something meaningful? Then again, is this a reader who freezes in the face of difficulty? All of this information will help you match students to books that will help them grow as readers.

	Name:_____				
Date	School- S Home- H	Title		Finished it!	Reread it!

Growing Stamina Every Day

Channel partners to share, first talking about their goals and how they read parts of books, and then reading those parts aloud.

"Readers, wow! Give yourselves a pat on the back! Tell your partner what your goal was and whether you met it!"

After children talked, I said, "Readers, when you are done talking about your goals, talk to your partner about *how* you read different parts of your books—and then you can take some time to try reading those parts to each other—and together, if you want."

Let children in on the secret that you have been timing their reading, and introduce a chart to track their progress across the unit.

Refer to the stamina chart.

"Readers, pat yourself on the back! As second-graders, your goal this year will be to read bigger, longer books—*and* to read for longer chunks of time. I made a chart so we, as a class, can keep track of how much reading you are able to do. Right here, on the bottom step, I wrote that for today, you were able to hold it together as readers for twenty-five minutes! That is five minutes more than you read yesterday . . . BRAVO! "And, at the top step, I've written the goal for the end of this unit: forty minutes. You can't just skip from reading for twenty minutes to reading for forty minutes, just like that!" I snapped my fingers.

"It helps to set step-by-step goals. So I'm going to suggest that tomorrow, you *try* to read for longer. And at home, try to do that too.

"Right now, will you take a minute to think of a few things you can do to help yourself keep going during reading time?" I put my finger on my temple to show I was thinking, and I encouraged the children to do the same. "Now share with your partner one or two or three things you will try tonight at home and tomorrow in school to help you read longer."

Session 4

Readers Read in Longer Phrases, Scooping Up Snap Words

MINILESSON

IN THIS SESSION, you'll teach children that readers run their eyes across the words on a page, looking for the ones they know in a snap. Then they can read scooping up longer phrases.

CONNECTION

Remind children of the work they've done recently to decide how a book wants to be read, and point out that sometimes hard words get in the way of this decision.

"Readers, you've been thinking about how books want to be read and then reading them in ways that bring out the feelings of the book. Some parts of books are written to be read in a soft, sweet voice, like this: 'Once upon a time in a land far, far away, lived a little old woman,' and some pages are written to be roared, not read, like this: 'I'll huff and I'll puff and I'll *blow* your house down!'

"When you were reading yesterday, I noticed that sometimes it is hard to concentrate on your reading voice, though, because there are just so many tough words everywhere! You look at the page and go, 'Gulp! There are a lot of new words here!' So instead of reading the page with feeling, you end up reading it like this":

> *Once/*
> *upon/*
> *a time/*
> *there/*
> *was/*
> *a ferocious/*
> *dog.*

GETTING READY

✔ Choose a page or two from *Katie Woo Has the Flu* (or whatever demonstration text you are using for this bend) that has lots of text, including a number of high-frequency words (see Teaching).

✔ Ask students to bring one book that they plan to read today to the meeting area for the minilesson (see Active Engagement).

✔ Keep a small-group planning page nearby to sort children into two groups for further instruction—one group to learn more high-frequency words and another to work on scooping up phrases quickly and smoothly (see Active Engagement).

✔ Display the anchor chart "Readers GROW Like Beanstalks!" on the easel and make sure the strategy "Read in BIGGER scoops" is ready to add to the chart (see Link and Share). 👆

✔ Prepare running records to continue assessing students (see Conferring and Small-Group Work).

✔ Display a copy of the nursery rhyme, book, or song *There Was an Old Lady Who Swallowed a Fly* for a shared reading (see Share). 👆

❧ **Name the teaching point.**

"Today I want to teach you that even when second-grade readers find a lot of tough words on a page, they don't fall back to reading one. Word. At. A. Time. There are always lots of snap words, words that they can read easily and right away, and they use those words to read in bigger scoops."

TEACHING

Model how you can look down a page and realize that even when a book has lots and lots of words, many of them are words you can read automatically.

"Readers, let's read *Katie Woo Has the Flu* together. You could look at this chapter and think, 'Whoa, this looks hard,' and you could start reading it. Like. This. But do *second*-grade readers do that? *No way*. Second-grade readers remember there are always a lot of snap words on the page." I paused. "Are there?" I asked, and as children answered I pointed to a few.

"Can we try reading this in bigger scoops? I'll go first, and then you take a turn." I opened up our demonstration text. "Wow! This might be hard. There are a lot of words here—but wait, we aren't scaredy-cat readers. We don't need to back down. Let's first find the words we know in a snap." I placed the page under the document camera.

> *"Ugh!" said Katie. "I don't want bugs running around in my tummy."*
>
> *"Not that kind of bug," said her mom. "A flu bug."*
>
> *"Good," said Katie. "But I still feel bad."*
>
> *"I feel hot, too," Katie moaned.*
>
> *Her mom took her temperature.*
>
> *"You have a fever," she said.*
>
> *"That's why you feel so hot. No*
>
> *school today! You are going back to bed."*

"Show me one finger if you see a word you know just like that." I snapped my fingers. "Show more fingers as you see more words you know in a snap!" Children held up their hands.

I glanced over at the children. I could see that a few of my highest readers were ready to pounce with, "That's not hard! I can read it!" But I motioned for children to listen and watch.

I began to read. Pausing at the start of the second line, as if overwhelmed, I then looked ahead and said, "Hmm, . . . I know this word, and this one. Wait! I know so many of these words right here. I can read them all together in a big scoop!" I read a line quickly, and then another.

> *"Ugh!" said Katie. "I don't want bugs running around in my tummy."*
>
> *"Not that kind of bug," said her mom. "A flu bug."*
>
> *"Good," said Katie. "But I still feel bad."*

Debrief in ways that accentuate the transferable work that you have done.

"Readers, did you see what happened? I found lots of words that I knew, and that helped me to read *more* and read *faster*. Scooping those words up together and reading in bigger scoops makes this reading feel faster and smoother."

You'll want to exaggerate your one-word-at-a-time reading to make it clear that choppy reading gets in the way of understanding.

FIG. 4–1 If many of your running records reflect the choppy reading seen here, this lesson will be especially important.

Demonstrate reading high-frequency words and whole phrases quickly. This will help you emphasize the fluency aspect of this lesson.

ACTIVE ENGAGEMENT

Invite children to look for words and phrases they know in a snap. Then ask readers to read the words they know to their partners in big scoops.

"Readers, let's try this right now. Take out the book you selected to read today. Open to the next page, and *before* you get overwhelmed, *before* you start to read, quickly run your eyes over the words." I waited as children started to do this. "Pop up a thumb . . . a finger . . . *more* fingers as you see words you know in a snap!" Children held up whole hands quickly, indicating that they knew many words on each page.

"Wow! Okay, now try looking for a bunch of words in a row that you know or almost know. When you've found some, read them to your partner, all together, fast and smooth!" I listened in as children read the phrases they found to each other.

LINK

Invite children to read an anchor chart aloud with you, reminding themselves of their growing repertoire of strategies. Add today's strategy to the chart.

"Readers, we already know that second-graders grow as fast as beanstalks; they can . . ." I pointed to each bullet on the chart, as children read aloud.

"And now we can add one more thing second-grade readers can do to grow like beanstalks." I added another strategy to the chart:

ANCHOR CHART

Readers GROW Like Beanstalks!

- Decide HOW to read.
- Give the book a sneak peek.
- Read more and MORE!
- **Read in BIGGER scoops.**

"Beanstalks, are you ready to grow some more? Fill out the reading logs you started yesterday, and then get started reading. Off you go!"

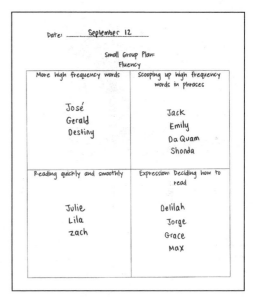

FIG. 4–2   Small-group planning sheet for fluency.

This is a great time to move around with a small-group planning page in hand. You can jot down names for two groups: one for students who need to learn more high-frequency words and another for children who need work on scooping up phrases quickly and smoothly.

Maximizing Opportunities to Assess

To REACH THE GOAL of matching all of your students to texts they can read by the end of this bend, you will want to use every moment and every spare hand to assess, assess, assess! If possible, ask a small group of kids to have lunch with you and another group to come early to school tomorrow. Ideally the principal will call, "All hands on deck," and recruit literacy specialists, classroom aides, student teachers—*anyone* who can help you manage your classroom while you assess your students during the first days of school. As long as you aren't sacrificing the goal of getting books kids can actually read in their hands, it is more important to get your first round of assessments done quickly than to get them done perfectly.

Although your primary focus will be on using running records to assess children's reading, there is also a repertoire of other assessment tools that you will draw upon as needed. Say, for example, your running records on Benjamin suggest that his comprehension and vocabulary skills are strong enough that they help him tackle words that are unfamiliar to him, but that whenever he attempts a word out of context, he gets stumped. His ability to rely on spelling patterns to read is very limited. You'll want to research Benjamin's letter/sound identification skills and his spelling, because these assessments will help you pinpoint the problem and help Benjamin get the help he needs.

You will want to keep a close eye on the children who seem to have slipped reading levels over the summer break. If children are currently reading from bins of books that represent last June's reading levels, it won't be challenging for you to notice the kids who seem to struggle with books they were presumably able to read at the end of the previous school year. With these kids, you may decide to postpone running records for a few days so that you have a little window of time to try to rub off the summer rust and get these readers back up to speed. Even if last June's books are a stretch, ask them to find some of those books that they remember well. First, suggest that they find titles in the library that they remember reading in June. With a sneak peek, help them recall as much as they can of those books. Then join them in reading these books, if you can. Try alternating pages, or try just reading the first two pages to the reader and then leaving the rest of the book with him to read independently. In these ways, you will give kids scaffolded help with levels that you suspect are, deep down, within reach for them.

MID-WORKSHOP TEACHING
Finishing One Book and Starting Another

Standing in the midst of the readers, I said in a voiceover, "Readers, lots of you are finishing one book and starting another. Before you start a second book, remember to add the new title to your reading log and then check the 'Readers GROW Like Beanstalks!' chart. It will help you remember to take a sneak peek—and to think, 'How does this book want to be read?'

"Readers, some of you are chatting about your books now, and I know that feeling of *needing* to talk about the funny parts and the sad parts and how those parts want to be read. But I'm going to ask you to save up that talk for now so you get some more time for reading."

Reading Faster and Smoother

Ask partners to listen super carefully to each others' reading, noting whether they are remembering to do all that they have learned about how second-graders read.

"Readers, let's gather in the meeting area for our share time today; record your reading on your log, then come to the rug and make sure that you are seated next to your partner." As the children gathered, I took out *There Was an Old Lady Who Swallowed a Fly*, and I placed our anchor chart right next to it. "I have a challenge. Will all our Partner 1s practice reading our song faster and smoother? As you read, I'm going to slide my pointer slowly under the words at first, but as you read on, I'm going to move my pointer faster sometimes and then faster still. Let's see if you can keep up while still remembering to do all the things you've learned to do." I gestured to our anchor chart.

> ANCHOR CHART
>
> ### Readers GROW Like Beanstalks!
>
> - Decide HOW to read.
> - Give the book a sneak peek.
> - Read more and MORE!
> - Read in BIGGER scoops.

"Meanwhile, Partner 2s, you will be researchers. Will you each hold a pretend clipboard and listen super carefully to your partner's reading? Pretend the anchor chart is a checklist, and check off Yes! if you see your partner deciding *how* to read, giving the book a sneak peek, reading more and more, and reading in bigger scoops.

"After, the 1s read this song, we'll switch. But, 2s, read whatever you have been reading today. Ready, Partner 1s? Start reading!"

There Was An Old Lady
Who Swallowed a Fly

There was an old lady who swallowed a fly
I don't know why she swallowed a fly—
perhaps she'll die!

There was an old lady who swallowed a spider,
That wriggled and wiggled and tiggled inside her;
She swallowed the spider to catch the fly;
I don't know why she swallowed a fly—
perhaps she'll die!

There was an old lady who swallowed a bird;
How absurd to swallow a bird.
She swallowed the bird to catch the spider,
She swallowed the spider to catch the fly;
I don't know why she swallowed the fly—

Keeping Tabs on Comprehension

IN THIS SESSION, you'll teach children that readers not only work to read more and more, but they also need to remember to *think* about their books. Reading *is* thinking.

GETTING READY

✔ Fold up a Post-it note on which you have written the teaching point (see Connection).

✔ Choose a couple of pages from Chapter 2 of *Katie Woo Has the Flu* or whatever demonstration text you are using for this bend (see Teaching).

✔ Ask children to bring one book each to the meeting area (see Active Engagement).

✔ Make sure the anchor chart "Readers GROW Like Beanstalks!" is ready to refer to, and be prepared to add the strategy "STOP, think, retell" (see Link).

MINILESSON

CONNECTION

Confess that last night you'd been too worried to sleep and had risen from your bed to write yourself a note to tell children something key. Use that story to drumroll the teaching point.

"Readers, I couldn't stop thinking about you last night. Our year is off to a great start. Already, you are taking charge of your reading. You are deciding not just *what* to read but also *how* to read, and you are working on reading more and more, on getting stronger and stronger.

"How many of you worked last night to read more and more, faster and faster, scooping up words?

"That's terrific. Give yourself a high-five!

"But I have to tell you something. Although I bragged to my family about how you are reading more and more and faster and faster, last night when I lay in bed, I started to worry. I couldn't sleep, I was so worried. So I got out of bed, went over to my desk, found a pen and a Post-it, and wrote myself a reminder to be sure to tell you something. You ready?"

I pulled a well-folded note out of my pocket. With great ceremony I opened it up and began to read aloud.

❖ **Name the teaching point.**

Reading from the now unfolded Post-it, I read, "Readers need to be careful not to get going, reading faster and faster, and forget to THINK about the story. They can keep tabs by stopping to make sure they can retell the events in order."

TEACHING

Explain that readers pause to check for comprehension. Recruit kids to stop you if you forget to think when reading the demonstration text—then do so, letting the children call, "Stop and think!"

"As readers push themselves to read faster and to read more, scooping up words in a snap, they also make sure to keep tabs on comprehension by checking in as they read, pausing at times to be sure they can retell the big events in order. Readers stop and think, 'What's happened so far?'

"Let's read from *Katie Woo Has the Flu*, making sure we THINK, stopping to retell what has happened so far. If we start to read faster and faster, more and more, without *thinking*—will you remind me? Give me a 'Stop, think, and retell!' signal." I made a stop sign with my hand, then tapped my head with one finger to turn that into a "stop and think" signal.

I picked the book up and placed it under the document camera, inviting the class to join me in a shared reading of Chapter 2, "Sick at Home." After a few pages, I stopped the class with my hand up like a traffic cop and said, "You know what? Our reading isn't feeling quite right to me." I scanned the room. "It looks like some of you agree. I see 'stop and think' signals. I have this weird sense that we are saying the words but not thinking about them. Let's take a comprehension check. Remember, reading is *thinking*. If you can't remember the story, it's almost like you haven't actually read it at all. Will you quickly turn and retell what happened so far in this chapter? Start at the beginning and retell the big events."

After a few moments, I called the class back. "I am so glad we stopped to do a comprehension check because that check told us we better go back and reread, this time making sure our brains are turned up high."

ACTIVE ENGAGEMENT

Prompt kids to take on roles in partnerships, taking turns reading from their own books and signaling a time to monitor for comprehension.

"Partner 1, will you read your book to Partner 2? And Partner 2, will you help Partner 1 remember to do a comprehension check? You can stop the reader, like this," I used my hand as a stop sign, "and then remind your partner to think. Get started. Then, switch roles. Partner 2, take the role of reader, and Partner 2, you be the one to put up a 'stop and think' signal."

Readers need to be careful not to get going, reading faster and faster, and forget to **THINK** about the story. They can keep tabs by stopping to make sure they can retell they can retell the events in order.

FIG. 5–1   The Post-it crumpled from my pocket.

Act out that you are just now, on the spot, coming to a dawning realization that something is amiss and you are reaching for a way to put your realization into words.

LINK

Remind children that reading is thinking, and nudge them to check their thinking by retelling what happened.

"Readers, it's time to read independently. Take a second to set a goal. How much will you read? How will you push yourself to get even stronger?" I gave them a minute to do this thinking. "And as you read, pretend you have the Post-it I wrote to myself last night." I pantomimed giving the note to each child—handing them out to one child, then another, and another. Many children clutched their fingers around an imaginary note, as did I.

"You may want to unfold that Post-it and put it on the desk beside your book." I pretended to do so, reading my note to them: "Readers need to be careful not to get going, reading faster and faster, and forget about comprehension. Readers can keep tabs by stopping, thinking, and making sure they can retell the events in order."

Refer to the anchor chart, on which you have placed the latest strategy.

"One way to check that you are thinking, comprehending, is to stop, think, and retell. Your reading time might go, 'Read, read, read, *stop*, think, and retell, then read, read, read again!' Let's all say that together this time." I counted the steps across my fingers this time, as children chimed in. "'Read, read, read, *stop*, think, and retell, then read, read, read, *stop*, think, and retell again!' Say it to yourself one more time, and when you think you've got it, take your make-believe reminder Post-it with you and get started reading! Today we are going to read for twenty-five minutes!"

ANCHOR
CHART

Readers GROW Like Beanstalks!

- Decide HOW to read.
- Give the book a sneak peek.
- Read more and MORE!
- Read in BIGGER scoops.
- **STOP, think, retell.**

STOP, Think, Retell.

read more

read 5 books today!

FIG. 5–2   Jude jots his reading goal on a Post-it.

Pushing All Readers Forward

B Y NOW, you will hopefully be able to look up from your assessments to do some teaching during reading time. If you are able to do so, you'll have two goals for conferring and small-group work today. First, you'll want to move quickly among the kids, doing everything you can to make sure the work of the new unit is underway. You've reminded your children to orient themselves to a book, push themselves to read a lot, and read in such a way that they can retell the text later. Those are really the most essential things about reading, so it will be important for you to make sure that your minilessons actually affect kids' actions.

The second thing you will want to do is to convene kids who are well below benchmark to make sure that they have access to this unit and, more importantly, that they are on a trajectory that promises to provide them with the support and instruction they urgently need. It is important to figure out the point at which these children's reading development became stymied. What can they do? What can't they do? For example, check whether these children are looking through the whole word. Perhaps they are not attending to the middle of the words or are having difficulty being flexible with the vowel sounds. Others might still be reading letter by letter, rather than chunking words into parts. If you find their command of these skills is shaky, chances are they are reading at level F or G. If you have a colleague who is teaching first grade, you might ask to borrow the *Readers Have Big Jobs to Do* unit, and ask yourself, "What aspects of this might be helpful for these kids?"

You will probably work with your well-below-benchmark students to make sure they have "texts under their belt" that they can read and reread with some independence. To provide them with those texts, you'll reread familiar songs, poems, and class books with them, working on things such as one-to-one matching, self-correcting when the matching doesn't come out even, using high-frequency words as anchor words, knowing an armload of high-frequency words, and using initial sounds to help readers cross-check. You might give this group of youngsters a more grown-up version of the reading pointers that kindergarten children so adore. If you have students reading at

level C, you'll also want to work on high-frequency words, building their own version of a word wall. You might spend another portion of time supporting these children's reading of unfamiliar texts at their instructional levels, with heavy text introductions, lessening the scaffolding over a progression of days.

MID-WORKSHOP TEACHING
Different Readers Need Different Goals

"Readers, you know that to be strong second-grade readers, you need to set goals for yourself and then push yourself toward those goals. And it is true that if you want to get better at something, you need to set goals. But I've been thinking about it, and I'm not sure that you *all* should set the goal to read faster and more. *Some* of you do need that goal—to read more and more, faster and faster, but some of you need the opposite goal! Some of you need to read more slowly and to pause more often to make sure your book makes sense.

"Right now, think which goal should be yours. You might look at your reading log and think about how many books you are reading each day. Or you might want to think about yesterday's share time when we read and your partner gave you feedback. What did your partner say you need to do?" Listing options on my fingers, I said, "One, read faster, read more? *Or* two, read slowly enough that you pause the story so it makes sense and you remember it afterward?"

After children thought for second, I said, "Make an imaginary road sign that can sit at the front of your desk. Does your road sign say, 'Go!' with an exclamation mark? Or does it say, 'Slow down'? What *does* it say?"

Note that these children blossom with consistency, so if it is possible for you or another teacher to meet with them in very small groups of three or four every day, even if only for ten minutes, that would be important. When you lead these small groups, you may want to keep a stopwatch with you and divide your time, so that one session contains several balanced literacy components that these kids need. Of course, these readers also need more time than they can get within the reading workshop, so hopefully you'll be able to provide additional time, and to make sure the work they do during that additional time is in sync with what you do with them during reading workshop.

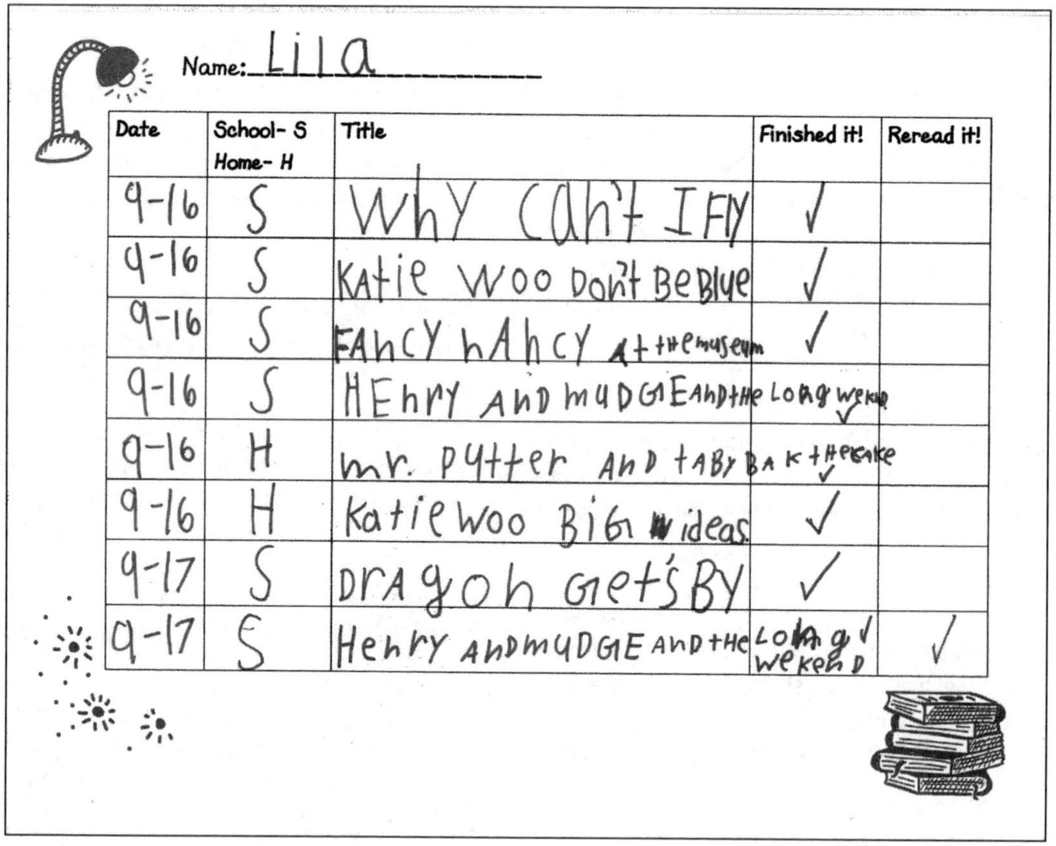

Name: Lila

Date	School- S Home- H	Title	Finished it!	Reread it!
9-16	S	Why Can't I Fly	✓	
9-16	S	Katie Woo Don't Be Blue	✓	
9-16	S	Fancy Nancy at the museum	✓	
9-16	S	Henry And Mudgie And the Long weken	✓	
9-16	H	mr. Putter And taby bak the cake	✓	
9-16	H	Katie Woo Big ideas	✓	
9-17	S	Dragon Gets By	✓	
9-17	S	Henry And Mudgie And the Long weken D	✓	✓

FIG. 5–3   Lila studies her log and sets a new goal.

Resolving to Read *More*

Praise children for the reading goals they set and accomplished and give them a new goal: to read more.

"Readers, as a class, you kept it together so that you were able to read for twenty-nine minutes—that is more than yesterday. You are definitely working toward the goal to read longer! I've got things to talk with you about, so can you come to the meeting area?"

Once children had convened, I said, "You are getting good at pushing yourself toward a goal. You pushed yourself toward the goal of reading longer today, and you also pushed yourself to read faster or slower or however you need to read. Since you are on a roll, this seems to be the moment for me to give you a new goal, if you are ready. You game?"

Most children nodded. Some feigned worry. "Here it is. The goal is to read . . . *more*!"

Invite children to be problem solvers, suggesting solutions to particular problems that get in the way of reading more, both inside and outside of reading workshop.

I was quiet, letting that goal sink in. I said, "It's easier to say than do, but here's the thing. Reading researchers say that almost nothing matters more than the amount of reading you do when you are your age. That's *huge*. So I thought we could try to come up with some tips for how to read more during reading workshop—but especially outside of reading workshop.

"I'm going to tell you some things that keep kids from reading a lot, and will you see if you can be problem solvers?

"Here's one problem: some kids read a lot when they have a book going, but when they finish the book, they take a long time to get started on another."

Hands shot up as kids suggested readers keep short stacks of books in waiting.

I pressed on with more problems: "Some kids have already read all the books at their level." "Sometimes kids keep losing their places." "Sometimes kids get stuck on a hard word." Together, the class and I came up with solutions to each of these problems, such as rereading, using bookmarks, and skipping the hard word and then returning.

"Readers, what I love is not just your solutions to these problems, but more—your mind-set that nothing, not anything, is going to stop you from reading up a storm. Way to go, second-graders!"

Second-Graders Can Mark Their Thinking with a Post-it

IN THIS SESSION, you'll teach your second-graders that grown-up readers stop often to think as they read. In fact, readers need Post-its to remember all the great ideas they might want to talk about with a partner.

GETTING READY

✔ Gather stacks of Post-it notes so they are ready for you to use (see Teaching), to give out to kids (see Active Engagement), and to place at tables (see Link).

✔ Choose a page or two from *Katie Woo Has the Flu*, or whatever demonstration text you are using for this bend, to model the work of marking places in a book that inspire thinking (see Teaching).

✔ Ask children to bring a pen or pencil to the rug (see Active Engagement).

✔ Display the anchor chart "Readers GROW Like Beanstalks!" so it is ready to refer to, and be prepared to add the strategy "Use stop & jots to remember ideas" (see Link). 👆

MINILESSON

CONNECTION

Tell a story that rallies kids to want to do the grown-up work of putting Post-its on places in books that need further discussion and thinking.

"Readers, when I was a kid, I had a babysitter who used to come over with a big bag of books to read. She always had a little stack of picture books to read to us and another stack of big, fat books, filled with Post-its and bookmarks, to read to herself after we went to sleep. I always looked jealously at those big, fat books, furry with Post-its. I couldn't wait until the day that I would be old enough to read books with Post-its. I begged her to let me use some of them. But she always said, 'You don't need Post-its. You're not old enough. Post-its are for grown-ups.'

"Well, guess what, second-graders? I have pretty exciting news for you. You *are* old enough to read books with Post-its!"

❖ **Name the teaching point.**

"Today I want to teach you that grown-up readers like you, who are reading longer books, have tons of ideas about their books—so many ideas, in fact, that they need Post-its to mark places in their books so they can go back to those ideas to talk and think more about them."

TEACHING

Demonstrate how when readers read, they retell parts to be sure they are understanding and pause to think and jot short notes on Post-its to hold on to thoughts worth sharing.

"Remember yesterday, how we learned that readers *stop*," and I held my hand up to gesture stop, "and *think*," I said, pointing to my head to gesture thinking, "as they read, and they make sure that they can retell the book? Well, today I want to show you that when you stop and think, you not only retell but you also *think* about things you want to talk about later.

"Readers, think along with me while I read a bit from *Katie Woo Has the Flu*. Let's see if we can think of an idea to talk about later." I read aloud a bit and then did a bit of retelling before I modeled having an idea worth sharing.

> When Katie woke up, her mom read her a story. It was about a girl with hair so long, she could jump rope with it.
>
> Her dad sang her a happy song.
>
> Katie drew a picture of the flu bug flying away from her.
>
> Katie's mom brought her hot soup and toast.
>
> "Ew, soup!" Katie moaned. "Ew, toast! I'm not hungry."

After reading just a few pages, I paused. "Wait! What's happening here? She is sick at home, taking a nap, right?" I put up a finger to track each part, motioning for children to do the same. "And then her mom reads her a story to help her feel better. And then her dad sings to her. Then her mom brings her some food." I paused here. "Wait, this is giving me an idea! I'm thinking the food looks good, but she says 'Ew!' Maybe she is still not feeling well. All that helping is not really working. Wow! We could talk about this with our reading partners later! I better mark this spot with a Post-it so that we don't forget!" I quickly wrote, "Still sick!" on the Post-it, and placed it in the book.

ACTIVE ENGAGEMENT

Channel students to listen while you read on, retell in their minds, push themselves to have a thought, and jot or sketch to hold that thought.

I quickly distributed Post-it notes to the students. "Readers, each of you has a Post-it so that you can try this out! I'll read a little more from *Katie Woo Has the Flu*, and when it's time to stop and think, will you remember what you've heard, retelling it in your own mind, and then push yourself to have a thought? Jot down that idea for us to talk about later, okay?"

I read aloud a bit more and then stopped and said, "Okay, let's first *stop* and *retell* (each of you in your own mind)." I left a moment of silence, and at the front of the room, did some silent retelling myself, putting up fingers to track each

Inviting children to make these gestures with you can dramatically increase engagement.

For now, don't get into elaborating on the kind of ideas you're having (for example, predictions or character work), because you'll teach all of that later in the unit and again in later units. For now, you are demonstrating simply the fact that when readers do have an idea, they find that it helps to place a Post-it note on the page to hold that idea, perhaps jotting a symbol or a few words to help them remember the idea later. Your goal in this demonstration is simply to show that readers not only retell but they also think, and when doing so, they are apt to generate ideas to discuss later.

FIG. 6–1 Bob jots an idea to talk about later.

part of the story. After a moment, I said, "Now let's *think*. Think to yourself, 'What ideas am I having? What could I talk about later?'" I paused, giving kids a few seconds of silence just to think.

"Thumbs up if you are having an idea." I saw many thumbs up, so I said, with urgency, "Quick—jot that on your Post-it so the idea doesn't float away. You want to hold on to it so you can talk about it later. I'm gonna just jot a word or two, aren't you? Some of you might make a little picture, a symbol, like a happy or sad face, or a question mark or whatever you want. You just need something that will help you remember your idea later. Let's call this a 'stop and jot' because that reminds you what to do. Stop and jot down an idea to remember."

As kids jotted on their Post-its, I got up from my seat, as always, to circulate and coach. I knew that today, there would likely be a few kids who would start to write full sentences, rather than a quick jot, so I kept an eye out. "Just a word or two, not the whole idea," I called out, voicing over to the whole class.

After no more than a minute, I said, "Great work, readers! I noticed lots of you using smiley or frowny faces, exclamation points, or question marks. Here's the question. Look at that Post-it. Pretend it's partner time. Does your Post-it help you remember your idea enough that you can share it?

"Try and see. Partners, talk about your ideas! Go!"

The room erupted into conversation, which I cut short, because the mission had been accomplished. The point of today's work was to show kids the value of having thoughts, holding on to them, and bringing them to book talks.

LINK

Channel children to apply what they've just done for *Katie Woo Has the Flu* to their own books, reminding them to stop, retell, and think about ideas, jotting their ideas on Post-its.

"When I call your table, please bring the Post-it you just wrote and stick it to the easel so we can marvel at them later, and then head back to your reading spots. There are Post-its for everyone to share at your tables, so when you're reading your own books, you will remember to stop, think, and retell. And when you have a great idea to talk about later, record it on one of those Post-its. Before long, your books are going to look just like my babysitter's books always looked—furry with Post-its!"

Remind children to refer to the anchor chart for reminders of all the other work they can do as readers.

"Now, before I send you off, is this the *only* work for you to do today during reading workshop? No, of course not! Grown-up readers, you can do more than one thing at a time! Use our chart to remind yourself of all the important work you can do today." I pointed to the chart, which I updated with the strategy about using stop-and-jots.

FIG. 6–2 Readers crowding around the chart to add their Post-its.

ANCHOR CHART

Readers
GROW Like
Beanstalks!

- Decide HOW to read.
- Give the book a sneak peek.
- Read more and MORE!
- Read in BIGGER scoops.
- STOP, think, retell.
- **Use stop & jots to remember ideas.**

Use stop & jots to remember ideas.

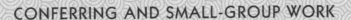
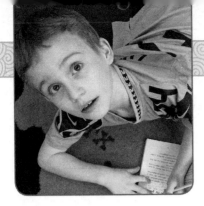

Using Post-its Productively

AS YOU CIRCULATE AROUND THE ROOM during independent reading today, a few predictable problems will likely arise. You've just introduced a brand-new and very exciting tool—Post-it notes! With anything new, kids are bound to overdo it, make mistakes, and find their own inventive uses for the new tool. You modeled jotting just a few words, but there will be kids who write way too much, spending too many precious minutes of reading time on their Post-its. You'll want to coach them to jot just a word or a picture clue instead. There will be others who flag every single page of their book—a wonderful sign of an engaged reader but also a clue that this reader needs help with determining importance. "Gosh," you might say, "you sure do have a lot of ideas to talk about with your partner! The thing is, we have only a few minutes of partner time, so one thing you can do is pick out just two or three of the most important Post-its and mark them with a star so that you'll know that of all the great ideas you're having, those are the most important." There will be yet others who invent their own ways of using the Post-its that you could not have predicted. Embrace their innovations, support their independence, and share their work if it's something from which other kids might benefit.

For readers not yet reading level H, you may want to gather them up and give them the option to use flags rather than Post-it notes to mark talk-worthy pages. There are some super-cute flaglike Post-its that will be enticing to kids, and the added benefit is that they leave no space for words. Chances are that your second-graders who are beginning readers are also beginning writers, and you may not want them laboriously spelling out their ideas on Post-its. Instead, the pages themselves can remind kids of their ideas. You may want to teach these youngsters some language for growing ideas: "I'm thinking . . . " "My idea is . . ." "This makes me wonder . . ."

Yesterday's conferring advice recommended that you start an ongoing small group of children who are well below the benchmark. You'll need to keep that work going. If you have a colleague who is teaching first grade, you will want to borrow the *Readers Have Big Jobs to Do* unit to learn strategies that are appropriate for pretransitional readers. Think of your work with this small group as a mini-version of that unit, tailored

for just the kids who need it. For example, today you might introduce some books at their instructional level. A strong book introduction provides an important scaffold that makes it possible for kids to have successful experiences reading books that they otherwise wouldn't be able to access.

In your book introductions, you'll want to give the gist of the story, pointing to a few key pictures and being sure to use key vocabulary in context. You'll also want to highlight the tricky parts; in level G books, for example, the words become increasingly difficult with irregular spelling patterns. You'll teach this small group of kids to use parts from known words to solve and read unknown words.

MID-WORKSHOP TEACHING
Having a Book Talk with Yourself

"Readers, I see so many of you using Post-its to hold your ideas. Bravo! You are definitely going to be ready to talk to your partners today!

"But I want to let you in on a little secret. Readers don't just talk to partners; they talk to themselves, too! You don't have to wait for share time to reread your Post-its. Instead, you can have a little book talk in your mind. In fact, try that right now.

"Go back to your first Post-it. Reread the page, think about the Post-it and the idea you had, and then try talking about it into your hand, so no one else can hear. You might say, 'I agree because . . . ,' and then point to places in the book that go with your idea. You might say, 'To add on . . . ,' and then say more. Then you can turn to the next Post-it and do the same thing. Go ahead!"

Turning Great Thinking into Great Conversation

Invite partners to share their thinking by talking off of their Post-its, and remind them of the role of each partner in a conversation.

"Readers, can you fill in your reading log and then bring the book you are reading with you, and come to the meeting area? I know that you are all really excited to share your thinking with your partner. Partner 1, you will go first. Please start by retelling your book before you talk about your ideas. Remember, you will want to use your Post-its to help you share your thinking." I made sure partnerships didn't just read their Post-its, but instead engaged their partners in their thinking. I coached kids to retell the marked part and then to explain the Post-it. I coached some partnerships to act out the part.

"Wow, look at the work you are doing! My old babysitter would be so impressed with the way you are using your Post-its to have conversations, to act parts out, and to share with each other! I wish I had been allowed to do this kind of thing when I was in second grade! How many of you plan to keep on using Post-its to keep track of your thinking, not just today, but every day?"

FIG. 6–3 Many teachers have a chart to keep track of which partner will go first.

Second-Grade Readers Roll Up Their Sleeves to Figure Out Tricky Words, Drawing on *Everything* They Know

IN THIS SESSION, you'll teach children that readers don't let tricky words derail them; instead, they roll up their sleeves, get down to work, and draw upon all they already know to tackle those words.

MINILESSON

CONNECTION

Establish reading partners—pairing like readers when possible—by using the new book baggies, strategically placed so that reading partners (or in a few cases, triads) sit side by side.

"Readers, today is a big day. It is a big day for many reasons. This morning you got a book baggie in which to store all the books you are eager to read soon. When you come to the meeting area, find your book baggie. That's where you'll sit. And find your name on our chart. There'll be another name on the chart—the name of someone who will sit beside you. That will be your partner, and the two of you will read together almost every day."

Once the children were all seated in the meeting area in their new assigned spots, I said, "Right now, use our Partner List chart to figure out which one of you is Partner 1 and which is Partner 2. Thumbs up if you are Partner 1. Great! Thumbs up if you are Partner 2. Great!"

Remind students of the ways they have grown as second-graders, and tell them that as they read longer books, they will encounter longer words.

"Earlier, we talked about all the ways that second-graders grow like beanstalks! You have later bedtimes. You get to watch new shows. And reading, too, has changed. You've already grown as readers. Now you each have a brand-new reading book baggie to hold books—books that you get to choose all by yourself! You get to choose not just *what* you'll read but also *how* you'll read. Your reading muscles will grow as you read longer, harder books. Remember, in this one year, you are going to go from reading books like this," and I held up *Fox on the Job* and *Katie Woo Has the Flu*, "to *this*," and I held up a Magic Tree House book and *Stink, The Incredible Shrinking Kid*.

- ✔ Prepare book baggies for each child by writing names, plus a "shopping list" that lets each child know how many books to choose. This will vary from level to level. Ask children to shop for books first thing when they get to school, before this lesson (see Connection).

- ✔ Use the book baggies labeled with names, now with books in them, to mark spots at the meeting area for kids to sit next to their reading partners during the minilesson (see Connection).

- ✔ Create a Partner List of assessment-based reading partners on chart paper and designate Partner 1 and Partner 2 (and Partner 3 for a triad) in each partnership (see Connection).

- ✔ Gather a few books of different levels to show the children a goal of growth. *Fox on the Job*, *Katie Woo Has the Flu*, a Magic Tree House book, and *Stink, The Incredible Shrinking Kid* are used in this session (see Connection).

- ✔ Gather a few familiar books to show children the kinds of tricky words they will encounter in their books. *Those Darn Squirrels*, *Captain Awesome to the Rescue*, and *Mrs. Jafee Is Daffy!* are used in this session (see Connection).

- ✔ Prepare the new anchor chart titled "When Words Are Tricky, Roll Up Your Sleeves!" (see Teaching and Share).

- ✔ Prepare to read a few more pages of *Katie Woo Has the Flu* or whatever demonstration text you are using and choose words to cover up that you think will be tricky (see Active Engagement and Share).

- ✔ Make sure students have access to individual white boards, dry erase markers, and erasers; or they could use paper to write on (see Share).

"The thing is, you don't just grow automatically. You have to work hard to grow. Sometimes reading is not so easy. You have to roll up your sleeves, say yourself, 'I can do this!' and get to work! The new books in your book baggie will give you the chance to practice reading longer books, and all that practicing will help you grow from *Fox*, to Magic Tree House, to *Stink*.

"Here's the thing: when you read longer books, you also end up reading longer words. Really! You are going to find words like these in your books," and I pointed to *geniuses* (or *approaching* or *determined*) in our read-aloud book, *Those Darn Squirrels*; *ferret* in Roy's *Captain Awesome to the Rescue*; and *mesmerizing* from Chrissy's *Mrs. Jafee Is Daffy!* "So for the next few days, we're going to practice being the kinds of readers who know what to do when things get tricky."

❖ **Name the teaching point.**

"Today I want to teach you that when second-grade readers come to a tricky word, they don't just say, 'Help me, help me!' Instead, second-graders roll up their sleeves and get to work! They draw on *everything* they already know to figure out that hard word."

TEACHING

Ask partners to recall the ways they know to figure out tricky words.

"Readers, for the whole upcoming bend in our unit, you'll learn about tackling tricky words. But before I can teach you *new* ways to figure out tricky words, I need to know what ways you *already* know. Partner 1, turn and tell Partner 2 what strategies you already know for solving tricky words!"

As partners talked, I crouched among them, listening to the strategies they named. Then I reconvened the class. "Nice work!" I said. "It turns out you already know a lot of things you can do when you encounter hard words." I revealed a new chart, titled "When Words Are Tricky, Roll Up Your Sleeves!" that listed many of the things I'd heard.

FIG. 7–1   You might choose to use magazine files instead of baggies to hold your readers' books.

Listen carefully to the strategies your students name. Although you have undoubtedly checked with first-grade teachers—and are aware of what children learned last year—it is revealing to hear the strategies children themselves name. Jot what they say and use this as an assessment to help you coach them later.

ANCHOR
CHART

When Words Are Tricky,
Roll Up Your Sleeves!

- Check the picture, and think, "What would make sense?"
- Use what's happening in the story.
- Look through the WHOLE word, part-by-part.
- Look for a word inside a word.
- Don't give up! Try something! Take a guess!

We quickly read through the list together.

ACTIVE ENGAGEMENT

Ask children to help you select a strategy from the list you compiled to solve a tricky word from the read-aloud.

"Ready to put your word-solving strategies to good use?"

The children nodded.

"Let's start. I've identified a word I'm pretty sure that most of you will find tricky. To make it extra tricky, I covered it up!"

I started to read and gestured for the class to chime in.

> Later, JoJo called Katie. "I missed you today! Miss Winkle says it's not the same without you."
>
> "Thanks," Katie _____.

"Right now, tell your partner what you think the word might be."

As children talked, I listened. Lots of kids suggested that Katie "said" thanks. Others pooh-poohed that idea, saying the word would be too easy. They said it would be *replied* or *cried*.

"Readers, I heard so many good ideas. Lots of you said that one way to solve this word is to use what's happening in the story to think about what would make *sense* here, so let's do that." I reread the sentence:

> "Thanks," Katie _____.

The covered word here is croaked. *Covering this word will allow you to prompt children to cross-check in multiple ways, since children who guess by using only the meaning will say* said. *Later, after you uncover the first two letters, children using only visual information at the beginning of the word will say* cried.

Here, your goal is to name for children what they are doing so that it is a replicable strategy. Notice how I repeat the strategy again.

"Hmm, . . . what makes sense? The word's quotation marks tell me that this character is *saying* something. That means that the covered word is a word that means how she is saying the word *thanks*. That helps us make a smarter guess, doesn't it? Let's see. I guess it could read, '"Thanks," Katie *said*' or maybe, '"Thanks," Katie *replied*.' Or because she is sick it could read, '"Thanks," Katie *whimpered*.' Or maybe, '"Thanks," Katie *croaked*.'

"Is it enough to think *only* about what might make sense? No way! What should we do next?" Pointing to one child as if he'd just supplied a next step, I nodded, and said, "Yes, yes, you are right. We look at the first letters." I peeled back the Post-it note covering the tricky word to reveal just the first two letters: *cr*. "Does that help? Can it read *said* if it starts with *cr*? Quickly turn and work on this together. How *is* Katie saying the word *thanks*?"

After a few seconds, I said, "Let's look at a little more of this word," and uncovered two more letters. After just a few more seconds, I called a partnership to come up and help. The duo pointed to the first four letters (*croa*), and read:

"*Thanks,*" Katie croa___.

At this point, kids were up on their knees, falling over themselves to call out that the word was *croaked*. "Readers, are some of you getting an idea of what this word reads? You are? Should we say our guess all together? Yes, okay, on three. One, two, three . . ."

"Croaked!" the kids shouted out. I nodded and gestured for them to read the whole sentence.

Continue to read aloud, and coach children as they think about how to figure out tricky words and then solve them.

"Okay, let's read on until we reach another tricky word—and when that happens, I want you to really roll up your sleeves and get to work using your strategies! Roll 'em up with me!" I pretended to roll up my sleeves.

We read on. Each time the children came to a tricky word, I prompted them to think about *how* to figure out the word before solving the word together.

LINK

Remind children of the repertoire of word-solving strategies they can use when they get stuck on tricky words in their books. Then send partners off to choose a reading spot next to each other.

"From now on, remember that you don't have to wait around for help; you can roll up those big-kid sleeves and use what you know to figure out those tricky words in your books.

"Today, when you head off to a spot for reading workshop, I have something special for you to do. I'd like you to choose a place to sit, so that you are next to your reading partner. You can sit back-to-back when it's time for reading on your own and then turn to sit shoulder-to-shoulder later, when it's time to work together. Choose wisely and carefully, because after today these will be your spots every day."

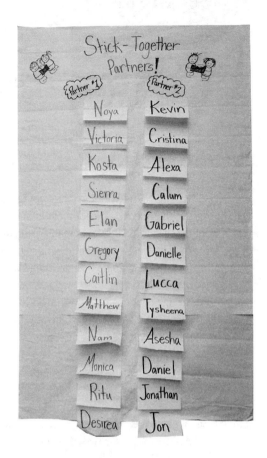

Choose words to cover up that you think will be tricky, but be sure that they are not all nouns. Nouns tend to be words that children can figure out from the picture alone. Choosing to cover verbs and adjectives pushes children to employ more strategies.

Launching Guided Reading

THIS IS THE FIRST FULL WEEK in which your students will hold baggies of just-right books, so this is a good time for them to buckle down to get a lot of reading done. You'll want to see kids doing a lot of reading and using all you have taught them to do. If you see a child preview a book without needing reminders—great! If you see a child monitoring for sense and going back to reread when a text gets confusing—great!

At the start of any new bend, you will need to spend a portion of your time rallying kids into the work of the bend, which means helping them be strategic word solvers. We describe that work more in the next session.

Although you will devote some of your time to supporting the work of the bend, the start of a second bend in a unit is also traditionally a time for you to lead one or more guided reading groups. And now, at the very start of second grade, this is certainly prime time for guided reading. After all, you have just launched kids into reading small collections of books at their assessed levels.

Your guided reading sessions will generally be ten minutes in length, like most of the small-group work that you lead. You may bring a timer with you to remind yourself to stay within time constraints. Like all of your small groups, the general plan will be that you talk with the kids for a minute or two; then they read as you circulate among them, commenting and coaching; and then you, again, talk to the group for a minute or two. Your guided reading groups will presumably involve four to six kids who read at the same level of text difficulty and who could use some support working with those texts. Often this will be a group of kids who are just moving up into a new level.

You'll begin with a book introduction, which many believe is the most important part of a guided reading session. Think of your introductions as being designed to support the meaning, syntax, and phonics children will encounter when reading a book. To support meaning, you can give children the gist of the story they will read. You can support the story's structure, too, perhaps using the formula "Someone . . . wanted . . . but . . . so . . . ."

For example, you might say, "This is a book called *The Little Red Hen*. In this story, the Little Red Hen finds a grain of wheat and decides she wants other animals to help her grow it and turn it into bread. But when she asks one animal after another to help her, they all say no!"

You might go so far as to say, "You know those books where one animal after another starts chasing someone? Well, this book is a bit like that. But in this book, the little hen doesn't chase one animal after another after another; instead, she goes to one animal after another to ask for help. Lots of books are organized like this one, in a list." Finally,

(continues)

MID-WORKSHOP TEACHING
Cross-Checking as You Problem Solve

"Readers, eyes up here a minute. I want to remind you of something that is essential to being a second-grade word solver. When you are trying to figure out a word, it's tempting to try one strategy, guess a word, and then pat yourself on the back and move on. But this can get you into trouble. Let me give you an example. Remember when I was reading *Katie Woo*? If I had just thought, 'It makes sense that the covered-up word is *said*. I bet the word is *said*,' I would have been in trouble. The very next line reads, '"Ribbit," JoJo croaked back.' I would not have understood that joke *at all* if I had just settled for my first guess, right?

"So I want to remind you that when you come to a tricky word, it's important for you to try one strategy and to cross-check with another. That means, try at least two strategies before you settle on a guess and keep reading. Hold yourself—and your reading partner—accountable to trying more than one strategy!"

your introduction will presumably support word solving. You'll call children's attention to a word or two (perhaps to *harvest*) and help them solve those words.

After the book introduction, children will read the book independently and you'll observe and coach, using lean prompts like "Does that sound right?," "Try it again. Think what would make sense," or "Does that make sense and look right?" When doing this coaching, move very quickly from child to child so that you can circle around to each reader more than once.

Regroup your students after they have read to talk about what happened in the story. Close your guided reading lesson by naming a teaching point that you frequently coached and prompted in this session. Remind students to try this often in their reading. You may suggest to your students to read this book one more time, thinking about the strategy as they reread.

Using All Your Strategies

Reinforce children's word-solving strategies by coaching them through the process one more time.

As I called kids over to the meeting area, I checked to be sure that they were filling out their reading logs on their own and then asked them to grab their white boards, dry erase markers, and erasers.

"Readers, I think you're ready to show off your word-solving strategies. Let's try this. I'm going to read on a bit in *Katie Woo Has the Flu*. Follow along. You'll see that I've covered another tricky word. I want you to roll up your sleeves to figure out that word, writing what you think is under the Post-it on your white boards! Follow along with your eyes and *think* to yourself, 'What would make sense here?' But don't write it yet." I projected the text and read:

> Then Pedro called. He told
>
> Katie, "When I broke my leg,
>
> _____ wrote funny things on my
>
> cast."
>
> "Lucky you," said Katie. "There
>
> is no cast with the flu."

Pointing to the Post-it note word, I said, "Are you ready to roll up your sleeves and get to work, readers? Roll them up with me!" I made exaggerated motions, rolling up my imaginary sleeves as the kids followed suit. Then I turned to reread the challenging sentence:

> He told Katie, "When I broke my leg, _____ wrote funny things on my cast."

"We could just sit back and *hope* the word gets solved." I slouched back in my chair and folded my arms. "But this is *second* grade! When the going gets tough, the tough get going!" I sat up tall to signal my resolve. "Are you already thinking about what strategies will help?" I pointed to the chart from earlier:

FIG. 7–2   A bin holding everything readers need to work, with white boards on the rug.

The covered word in the projected text is every-one. Again, this is a word that will require children to cross-check in multiple ways.

"Go ahead and use whatever strategy you think will help and write down the word you think it could be. Check the picture and think, 'What would make sense?' Use what's happening in the story.

"Wow! Excellent work. I see some kids wrote *people* or *everyone* or *everybody* or *kids*. All of those make sense. It has to be a word that shows that people wrote funny things. It can't be a random word like *car* or *duck*, right? Let's look at the first letters now so you can check what you wrote." I peeled off a bit of the Post-it to reveal the first two letters: *ev*. "Go ahead, double-check. If you wrote a word that doesn't start with /ev/, think 'What else would make sense here?'

Some children erased their word and wrote a new one. "Nice, but it could be something we would have never thought of, so we need to look through the whole word, part-by-part." I peeled off the rest of the Post-it and gave kids time to confirm or fix their word.

By having kids write a word using only context clues, you are able to informally assess how well they are able to use this strategy.

Readers Use More Than One Strategy at a Time

Figuring Out What Makes Sense and Checking the First Letters

IN THIS SESSION, you'll teach your students that to become flexible word solvers, readers often need to use multiple strategies at the same time. Specifically, this minilesson highlights using meaning first to make a good guess and then using the print (visual/graphophonic information) to cross-check.

GETTING READY

✔ Display the anchor chart "When Words Are Tricky, Roll Up Your Sleeves!" so that it is ready to refer to (see Connection).

✔ Prepare tricky words (in isolation and in sentences) on sentence strips (see Connection, Teaching, Active Engagement, and Mid-Workshop Teaching).

✔ Tell children to bring their book baggie with them to the meeting area (see Link).

✔ Place Post-its in table bins for marking tricky words (see Link and Mid-Workshop Teaching).

✔ Prepare individualized goal cards for each student (see Conferring and Small-Group Work).

✔ Display the anchor chart "Readers GROW Like Beanstalks!" (see Share).

MINILESSON

CONNECTION

Remind students that this new bend of the unit focuses on word solving by checking in on whether they've been doing good work on that front.

"Readers, have you been finding words that take some work in your books?" I scanned the room, glad for enthusiastic nods. "That's second grade for you!" I said. "Am I right that sometimes you need to work at figuring out how to pronounce them, and sometimes you need to work at figuring out what they mean? Are you remembering that you have a lot of strategies for tackling those hard words? Quick, tell each other which of these strategies on the anchor chart you have been using a lot!" (See next page.)

Suggest to children that you've been thinking about how to help them become more powerful word solvers, and talk up the importance of flexible use of their strategies, giving them a chance to practice.

"Readers, yesterday you not only learned that you have lots of ways you can work on solving hard words, but you also learned that in second grade, you need to be flexible word solvers. For example, if you were trying to say this word," I said as I wrote *picturesque*, "it would be important that you try it one way, then another way, then another, using all those strategies on our list.

"Before you learn yet more techniques, try using these strategies to figure out this nice juicy hard word. You game?" I hung a sentence strip containing the word *picturesque*:

The view of the rolling hills and the farms was picturesque.

"Partner 1, turn to Partner 2 and do your best work to read this sentence to your partner. Partner 2, if your partner gets stuck, you could use the chart to remind your partner of some strategies to try. Be flexible." The children solved the sentence, working together, and I admired the fact that they drew on all they knew.

You'll want to get your students talking about the strategies they use. While you'll want to keep the sharing in your connection brief, you can also learn a lot from listening in a bit.

❖ Name the teaching point.

"Today I want to teach you that to become flexible word solvers, one of the tricks readers use is to use two strategies *at the same time!* Specifically, it helps to reread a sentence and to think about what word probably goes in that spot and then check it by reading the first chunk of a word."

TEACHING

Point out that although it is not easy to do two things at once, it is useful to use more than one strategy at a time when word solving.

"Readers, can any of you pat your head and rub your stomach at the same time?" I tried it, and so did the kids, with little success. "It's hard, right? Well, the work I am going to teach you today is hard in just that same way. The trick is that you have to do several things at once.

"I know you have heard of this before, but it is becoming super important now that you are second-graders and growing into such grown-up books. Have any of you noticed that the words in your books are becoming looooooooooong and hard? What are some hard words you have been reading lately?"

Kids called out words: *spaghetti, encyclopedia, salamander*.

Model how you solve a tricky word by thinking about what would make sense and looking at the first chunk of the word.

"So let's take a word like one of those and try doing two things at once," I said, patting my head and rubbing my stomach to illustrate. "Watch how I solve this tricky word. I need to do *two* things at once! *First*, I'll reread the sentence and think about what word would make sense. *Second*, I'll double-check my guess by looking at the first part of the word. Then I'll put the two things together: I'll reread the sentence again and run right into that tricky word so that it pops right out! You ready to watch? Here is the word," I said and wrote *tentacles*. "And, here is the sentence."

The octopus reached its long <u>tentacles</u> into the next fish tank.

"First, I'm rereading and thinking really hard about what might make sense. 'The octopus reached its long . . . something or other . . . into a fish tank? Um, it's got to be like part of his body, a long part. Now I'm going to double-check with the first chunk of the word." I pointed to the first part of the word and read /ten/.

Transitional readers will encounter increasingly difficult words as they read. While children are often tempted to tackle the letters first, proficient readers keep meaning at the front of their minds at all times.

"Second, let me reread the whole thing and run right into the tricky word so that it might pop right out of my mouth." Putting these together, I reread ". . . reached its long . . . /ten/ . . . *tentacles*! That's it. Tentacles!"

ACTIVE ENGAGEMENT

Invite children to work with a partner to solve a couple of tricky words, using two particular strategies at once.

"You ready to try again?" I asked. "Again this time, work with your partner to word solve the tricky word. Remember to do two things at once. Reread the sentence with your thinking cap on, trying to figure out what might go in that spot, *and* chunk the word into parts: read the first part, then the next. See if—presto!—the word comes to your mind.

"Before I post the sentence, can I ask you and your partner to whisper into your hand super quietly so you don't give the word away to others and ruin the fun?" I asked, and then taped a prewritten sentence strip onto the easel, reminding children to read the sentence once, thinking, "What word would make sense here?"

The wizard waved his wand over the toad and said, "Abracadabra," and the toad turned into a princess.

Some guessed the word before they even began looking at the first part of it, and I revealed a second sentence.

I built a little home for the tiny red salamander, hoping to match its home environment.

The kids had a lot of success with the first word, though one or two challenged the fact that it wasn't a real word. Some needed help on the second word.

Debrief, naming the importance of being flexible when encountering tricky words.

"Readers, the main thing I'm hoping you see is that when you come to tricky words, you need to be *flexible* word solvers. You can't just throw up your hands and say, 'Help me, help me!' Not in second grade. No way!"

LINK

Congratulate children on their independent word-solving growth.

"Readers, when I thought about how to design this unit so that it got you off to a really powerful start on this amazing year for reading growth, I knew it would be important to spend some time making

Don't belabor this. The kids need chances to do this work more than they need to hear you talk about it. Just model enough to let them know that there are two strategies at once here.

FIG. 8–1 A sentence strip on the board can easily display the practice sentence.

FIG. 8–2 This running record shows a reader who over-uses visual information, forgetting to make reading make sense. This lesson will help you address that struggle.

sure that everyone in this class is willing to work hard to solve tricky words. Back when you were first-graders, some of you might have just waited for help, saying, 'Can you help me? Can you help me?'

"Already I can tell that this is a class of powerful problem solvers. I'm thinking about that saying, 'When the going gets tough, the tough get going.' You ready to get going?"

Ask children to choose the book in their book baggie that seems the hardest and to skim through it for words that may pose challenges, perhaps marking those with Post-its.

"Before you head off, look through your baggie for your hardest book, the one that is the most likely to give you some tough going, and skim through that book, alert for any words that might pose an exciting challenge for you. Once you see some tough going ahead, then—get going! You can read any book in your baggie—but don't just start at the hard words, even if you want to! Start at the beginning."

As the kids settled down in their reading spots, I reminded them, "You might want to mark the challenges you find with a Post-it so that you can share them with each other later."

Here we very deliberately make the challenge of a hard word sound fun. When children view challenges as fun, they develop the mindset they need to grow.

Building Momentum in Your Small Groups

BY NOW you will presumably have started a guided reading group or two. These small groups should probably meet every day or on alternate days in strings of three or four lessons so that you are able to build up some momentum.

You can use these guided reading groups to show kids how to orchestrate strategies—using multiple strategies—but you can also angle them to support more specific goals. For example, if a review of your data suggests to you that students need more vocabulary and more strategies for figuring out the meaning of unfamiliar words, you can bring that forward in a guided reading group. On the other hand, if a particular group of readers needs support thinking about what is happening in the story, you can angle your guided reading so you support students to stop and list the events in a story across their fingers.

In addition to leading one or two small groups, you will want to work with individual readers. One way to reach many students is to sprinkle the classroom with a few compliment conferences by simply plopping yourself alongside a table of readers, and then you watch for something to compliment. To one table of kids, you might say, "I see everybody at this table using the chart to remember all the strategies you might use for solving tricky words. That's terrific!" To an individual, you might say, "I see you still using Post-its, just like we learned last week! That's awesome! You may want to record just a word or two that will capture some of the ideas you had while reading, because other kids are definitely going to want to hear your ideas."

There will surely be a few children whom you want to support with stamina and focus, as well. For these children, continue setting volume goals, as you did with the whole

---

MID-WORKSHOP TEACHING **Welcoming the Work of Tackling Hard Parts, Using Two Strategies at Once**

"How many of you have found some tough going while you were reading today?" I asked. When hands shot up, I raised a fist triumphantly and called, "Waa-hoo! Good going. Are you marking those hard parts? If not, look back over what you have read and mark the hard parts, because at the end of today, you may want to share them with each other.

"If you aren't finding enough hard words in your books and you want some extra challenges," I said, "I'm leaving some sentence strips up here, in three piles: hard, harder, hardest. You could take any one of these if you aren't finding a lot of hard words in your books. Remember, when you come to hard words, you may need to . . ." I paused to pat my head and rub my stomach and finished my sentence, "do two things at once."

---

class in the first bend. This is a great time to remind students to track their reading and to set goals for themselves, using the reading logs you established earlier. Alternatively, if some students are struggling with reading logs, you might ask them to jot a number on a Post-it to indicate how many books they plan to read today. As these children read, they can keep a tally underneath that number—making their goals and their work visible as you walk around. You can quickly check the Post-it to provide encouragement.

Now that you have assessed all your children, you can also start to give them individualized goal cards. These are personalized charts that help children focus their reading efforts on strategies that you have taught explicitly. When you meet with a child—in a conference or small group—you can add a Post-it to the goal card with the strategy that was the focus of your teaching. This goal card will act as a reminder for the student and can travel with that student in her book baggie. Thus, when the child reads at home, she will be reminded of her goals, and her parents will also become aware of those goals. Additionally, the goal sheet can travel with the student to support teachers, acting as a form of communication between teachers, as well as a document to support skill/strategy transfer in the various settings where she reads.

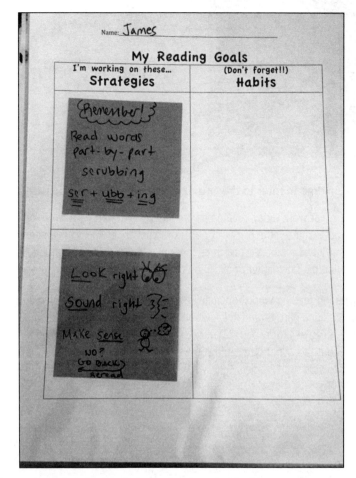

FIG. 8–3 Use a goal sheet to help readers keep track of your teaching. Write a focused strategy on a Post-it during a conference or small-group work, then leave it with the reader as a reminder. You can update the sheet when you see progress.

Remembering All the Work to Do When Reading

Remind children to refer to the anchor chart to find work to do with a partner.

"Readers, great work today, rolling up your sleeves and getting to work on the tricky parts in your books. A lot of you even took a sentence strip or two for an extra challenge. *And* you've been reading a little more each day. Today, you read for thirty-two minutes—just three more minutes and you'll be at the next step on our stamina chart. You're going to be reading big fat chapter books in no time if you keep working hard and growing like this!

"Today during reading workshop, many of you chose to flag some of your tricky words so that you could share them with your reading partner, and in a few seconds, you'll have time to do that. But first, I want to ask you a question: What if you didn't flag any tricky parts? What else can partners talk about or work on together? I could tell you, but I want you to think about this. What else could you and your partner do together? Think about all that you've learned this year." I motioned toward the "Readers GROW Like Beanstalks!" chart. "Tell your partner."

> **ANCHOR CHART**
>
> ### Readers GROW Like Beanstalks!
>
> - Decide HOW to read.
> - Give the book a sneak peek.
> - Read more and MORE!
> - Read in BIGGER scoops.
> - STOP, think, retell.
> - Use stop & jots to remember ideas.

Listen in as children consider options, and guide them to make a plan for the work they'll do today.

As kids talked about choices for working with partners, I listened in and noted some of their responses. After a few moments, I stopped them and shared out some of the choices: Readers can talk about their ideas. They can recommend good books to their partners. They can help each other with the tricky parts that they flagged in their books.

"Now decide what you'll do today and get going. You've got plenty of work to choose from."

Session 9

Some Beginnings and Endings Can Be Read in a Snap!

In earlier sessions, we've provided tools and methods that inform your teaching. Occasionally, as with this session summary, we suggest you work more independently.

MINILESSON

In the connection, you might celebrate that you saw some students tackling really long words by chunking them, part by part. Then, as an invitation for kids to strut their stuff, you can say a sentence leading up to a long word and hold up an index card on which you have written that one challenging long word, using your hand or another index card to channel readers to proceed chunk by chunk. Repeat this with a few words. Be sure that your challenging words contain the prefixes *pre-* and *un-*, and some common endings.

> Last night for supper we ate <u>pre/cook/ed mac/a/ron/i.</u>
>
> Last night for supper we ate <u>un/cook/ed mac/a/ron/i.</u>
>
> Our book ended <u>splen/did/ly.</u>

For the teaching point you might say, "Today I want to teach you that when second-grade readers read words part by part, they know that lots of words use the same beginnings and endings, which they can read in a snap, just as if they are snap words."

During your teaching, return to some of the words from the earlier work and point out that there are some word parts that are easy to read because they are almost like snap words. They appear often so that readers look at them and think, "Oh, I know that!" Those parts sometimes come at the starts of words and sometimes at the ends of words.

With your class, collect lists of words with common beginnings (such as *prepare, premade; unmade, undo*) and words with common endings (such as *walking, sleeping; softly, quickly*), but do not aim for especially long lists, because these can grow throughout the day and the unit. But do aim to include in the list the prefixes and the word endings that you'll soon ask kids to tackle.

SESSION 9: SOME BEGINNINGS AND ENDINGS CAN BE READ IN A SNAP!

51

Then choose a page in your demonstration text that includes words with inflected endings. The first few pages of Chapter 3 of *Katie Woo Has the Flu* provide lots of opportunities for this work. Display the page and invite children to work on it alongside you.

Katie took another little nap.

When she woke up, she felt a lot better.

Her mom brought her more soup and toast.

"Yay, soup!" Katie said. "Yay, toast! I'm <u>starving</u>!"

"I'm <u>feeling</u> more like me," Katie said. "It feels good to feel good!"

That night, Katie <u>dreamed</u> that her class sang a "Welcome Back" song to her.

In the active engagement, you might channel children to work on paying attention to word endings in some text from a different source. You could use a paragraph or two from a favorite read-aloud book or a stanza from a poem. You will probably want to highlight the words with inflected endings. Then invite Partner 2 to read as Partner 1 listens for word endings.

In the link, remind readers that using a variety of strategies will help them read even the trickiest words. Recall the anchor chart "When Words Are Tricky, Roll Up Your Sleeves!" You can say, "Yesterday, you learned that to be flexible word solvers you might need to use more than one strategy at the same time. From now on you might try one way to figure out a word, and then another way, *and* I hope you won't forget to check those beginnings and endings, too!"

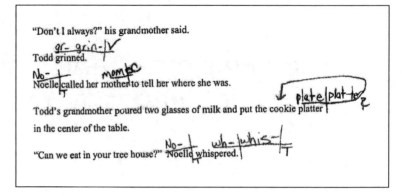

FIG. 9–1 This running record reveals that the reader is not using endings to help him decode. This lesson will be of particular importance in classrooms with such readers.

CONFERRING AND SMALL-GROUP WORK

As you pull small groups today, you might choose to work with a group of children who have not built a significant bank of high-frequency words. In a small group, you could teach the children not only a few new words but also how to teach themselves some of these words, using the strategy that is sometimes referred to as Look Read Spell Write Look Read, which is taught during the kindergarten unit called *Super Powers*.

This quick little routine will teach children to first *look* at a word, noticing how many letters it has and its shape, and then to *read* the word out loud. Next, they *spell* the word, perhaps chanting it several times, and then they *write* it. Finally, children *look* at and *read* the word again to be sure they wrote the word correctly. Let the group go through this routine with each word and then read independently a book or two from their baggies, pushing to read each word automatically.

Mid-Workshop Teaching

In your mid-workshop teaching, remind children that looking closely at the endings of words doesn't mean looking just for *ed* and *ing* endings. Point out that *er*, *s*, and *es* endings can also be added to words, so children should read the alert for whatever kind of ending will make a word sound right and make sense. You can post a few examples to illustrate. When you read these together, try each word without the ending to point out how it sounds.

> *There are so many pie<u>s</u>.*
> *I called over to the police offic<u>er</u> to ask him for help.*
> *I love when my dog kiss<u>es</u> me on my face.*

SHARE

Today's share session could be a good time for children to practice listening for when reading does not sound right. Take a paragraph from any book in the library and ask children to listen as you read. You might say, "Readers, I'm going to read a bit from this book, and I'm going to be the kind of reader who forgets to read the endings of words. When you hear a part that doesn't sound right—because I left off an ending—will you put up a stop hand? Then you'll have a chance to work with your partner to fix my reading!"

Chapter One
The Writer

Catina wanted to be a writer.

Every evening after dinner, she would make herself a cup of ginger tea and sit down to write another chapter in her book.

1

Don't Forget the Middle!
*Readers Are Flexible When They Encounter
Vowel Teams in Tricky Words*

IN THIS SESSION, you'll teach children that readers pay close attention to the middle of tricky words and are flexible when they encounter vowel teams, using what they know about the variety of sounds a vowel team might represent to help them read.

GETTING READY

✔ Provide a white board, marker, and eraser, or paper and writing implement, for each child and for yourself (see Connection).

✔ Prepare a list of vowel team words to sort into long and short vowel sounds (see Connection).

✔ Prepare twenty index cards with words that contain the vowel teams *oo, ou,* and *ee* (see Teaching).

✔ Hang a pocket chart near the meeting area to place the index cards in (see Teaching).

✔ Prepare a page from Chapter 3 of *Katie Woo Has the Flu* by highlighting several examples of vowel teams (see Active Engagement).

✔ Ask children to bring a just-right book to the minilesson (see Active Engagement).

✔ Display the anchor chart "When Words Are Tricky, Roll Up Your Sleeves!" and be ready to add the strategies "Reread and ask, 'Does that sound right?'" and "Use vowel teams, and ask, 'Would a different sound help?'" (see Link).

✔ Place small Post-its at each table, or in each child's book baggie, for playing "Guess the Covered Word" (see Share).

MINILESSON

CONNECTION

Channel students to do some word work on their white boards, recording words in categories based on whether the vowel team makes a short *e* or long *e* sound.

As children convened in the meeting area, I gave each a white board, a marker, and an eraser. "Readers, or shall I say *writers*, because in this session you will be both. Let's set up our white boards to do some long vowel work. To set up your board, will you please draw a line down the middle, and write the word *beach* at the top on one side, and *head* on the other?" I set up my own white board to look just like the kids'.

beach   I head

"We know that some vowels go together in words and make sounds, usually making the sound of the name of the first vowel. Those are vowel teams. When I was little, my second-grade teacher taught me, 'When two vowels go a-walkin', the first one does the talkin'. But sometimes, those vowel teams are tricky! Sometimes the first vowel doesn't do the talkin'! You have to watch out for those tricky vowel teams. Every time you see two vowels together, you can think to yourself, 'Hey, I know you, you tricky vowels—and you're *not* going to trick me!'

"Here's a tricky vowel team that you probably already know about: *ea*." I underlined the *ea* in the words *beach* and *head* on my own white board.

b<u>ea</u>ch   I h<u>ea</u>d

"You are going to sort some words on your white boards. You'll write all the words that make a long ē sound, as in *beach*, on one side. You'll write all the words that make a short e sound, as in *head*, on the other side." As I read each word from my list (*reach, dream, death, beast, spread, bread, teach, steam, dead, seat*), I gave kids a moment to write the word on their boards, and then wrote the word on my own board so they could check their work against mine.

beach	head
reach	death
dream	spread
beast	bread
teach	dead
steam	
seat	

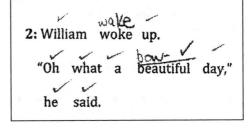

FIG. 10–1   Children can use their white boards to sort words by listening for short- and long-vowel sounds.

"Great work! Do you see how vowel teams, like *ea*, can be super tricky? All of these words are spelled with *ea* and they *look* like they should sound the same, but they don't sound the same when we read them, do they? You might have to try one sound and then another to figure out a word. Take a minute right now to circle all the vowel teams. Do you notice something? Are these tricky vowel teams at the beginning of the word? Are they at the end of the word? Where are they? Yes! You noticed it. These words all have tricky vowels teams right in the middle, where they are the hardest to spot! That makes them *even trickier*! Keep an eye out for those tricksters!"

❖ **Name your teaching point.**

"Today I want to teach you that readers sometimes have to work *extra* hard to figure out the middle of a word. Readers keep an eye out for those tricky vowel teams that can make different sounds. Readers know they may need to try one sound and then another to figure out a word."

TEACHING

Invite students to read words that contain vowel teams off of index cards.

"Readers, we have already practiced writing some tricky vowel team words. Now let's read some words with super tricky vowel teams in the middle. Sometimes the vowel team will make one sound in one word and a different sound in another word, which makes them extra tricky! Whenever you see two vowels together, you can say, 'Wait a second, you can't fool me!' Are you ready to roll up your sleeves?"

Of course, sometimes vowel teams do appear at the beginning or end of a word, but today's lesson is all about the middle—where word solving tends to be the most challenging.

```
2: William  woke  up.
   "Oh  what  a  beautiful  day,"
   he  said.
```

FIG. 10–2   When children are not flexible with vowel sounds, meaning begins to break down.

I held up about twenty cards for students to read, each with a word containing a vowel team. Seven words included *oo*, seven *ou*, and six *ee*. At least one word for each vowel team had an atypical sound.

> hoot, brook, soothed, gloom, spooked, footing, books
>
> could, cloudy, grounded, shouting, would, sprouted, shouldn't
>
> queen, sleep, green, beet, feel, been

The children read each one out loud, while I occasionally coached them to try more than one sound in the middle—sometimes even when they pronounced it properly first—so that they would get used to the act of checking to make sure a word is correct. I placed each card they read in a pocket chart.

"Wow, readers! You didn't just work harder to figure out those words. You were also *flexible*. You tried different sounds until each word sounded correct. Bravo!"

Lead students in a sorting activity to highlight the different sounds a vowel team can represent.

"Let's try another challenge. Let's sort these words to help us name the particular sounds these vowel teams can make. Which team should we start with?" Children called out their preferences, and I quickly responded, "Sounds like we should start with *oo*! As I hold up each word, read it and then say, 'The *oo* sounds like . . . ,' and then say the sound. Ready?"

The class cheered.

I quickly pulled all the *oo* cards out of the pocket chart and cleared away the rest of the words, so that I could display the words in two columns. I held up the first word. "Books!" the class shouted.

"The *oo* sounds like . . . ," I prompted.

The class responded, "/o͞o/!" I held up the words *brook* and *footing*, and the children quickly indicated that those words had the same medial vowel sound as *books*. Then I held up *soothed*. There was a hesitation and a bit of chatting before everyone decided that the *oo* here sounded like /o͞o/. I made a new column for *soothed*. We went on to sort more words—*hoot*, *gloom*, and *spooked*—checking the vowel sounds before placing them in columns.

"Wow! That was some hard work. That *oo* vowel team really can be tricky!"

Continue the sort with a few more vowel teams.

"Let's practice with our other vowel teams, too!" I repeated the sorting process again, this time with *ou* words, including *could, cloudy, grounded, shouting, would, sprouted*, and *shouldn't*. Then we moved on to the *ee* words: *queen, sleep, green, beet, feel*, and *been*.

You may have noticed that in the connection, we used long/short vowel patterns, and here we're using some ambiguous vowel patterns, like ou, oo (others include ow and oi), and another that typically represents long vowel sounds ee (others are ea, oa, ai). We began, in the connection, with work that is generally easier and more familiar, and then here, in the teaching, we upped the ante a bit. If your students are reading at levels I/J, you might choose to stay focused on the typical long vowel/ short vowel teams. However, if your students are reading higher levels, you might choose to study more words with ambiguous vowels— vowel teams that are neither long nor short. More challenging examples include should, thought, *and* drought.

FIG. 10-3   You can use index cards and a pocket chart to quickly sort words with vowel teams that represent more than one sound.

ACTIVE ENGAGEMENT

Invite children to be flexible as they use vowel teams to read words in context.

"Well, you certainly are working hard with vowel teams when you are reading words off of *cards*, but can you take on this challenge when you are reading a *book*? Get ready to grow. Let's try!"

I put up a page from the demonstration text on the document camera and pointed to a few highlighted words. "Let's read this part from *Katie Woo Has the Flu* together. Notice I've highlighted a few words that have vowel teams. When we get to them, you will have to work hard to figure them out. Ready?"

> *Miss Winkle played the* <u>*tambourine*</u> *and did a happy dance.*
>
> *A few days later, Katie went back to* <u>*school*</u>*.*
>
> *Her friends welcomed her with a song.*

Each time we reached a highlighted word, I stopped the children to confirm that they had read it correctly, asking if the word sounded right and, if not, would a different sound help? I also encouraged them to name the sound the vowel team represented in the word.

Remind readers of the importance of flexibility in the moment of reading. Invite them to read with their partner, searching for opportunities to practice with vowel teams.

"Readers, right now, practice this with a partner. Partner 1, will you pull out your book and start to read to your partner? Partner 2, listen and read carefully beside your partner. Any time you see a vowel team, stop your partner and check that your partner is flexible in figuring out the tricky words. When you figure out a tricky word, check it by rereading the sentence and asking, 'Does that sound right?' If it does, then keep on reading. If it doesn't, try a different sound. Go ahead!"

I moved from partnership to partnership, listening and coaching as kids read. I prompted them to check their reading of vowel teams but did not limit myself just to this work, knowing that this was a quick opportunity to make sure children were using all their strategies.

"Wow! Readers, you certainly are finding a lot of places to work on those vowel teams!"

Don't worry if some of the words you have highlighted are not particularly tricky for the class as a whole. The point of this work is to get kids trying different sounds when they see vowel combinations, so that when the word is tricky they will have experience to draw from.

LINK

Send children off to read, reminding them to use all they know about vowel teams as they read their own books.

"So, readers, as you go off to read, most of the time you will be reading your books, nice and smoothly, with expression. You'll be lost in deep thought as you picture the story and enjoy your books. But every once in a while, there will be a tricky word, and that's when you'll need to roll up your sleeves and remember everything you know about figuring out those tricky parts."

I added the new strategies to the chart, and then we read it all together:

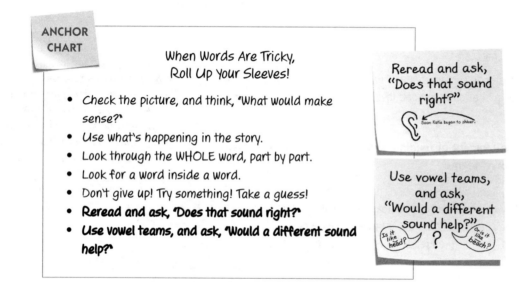

ANCHOR CHART

When Words Are Tricky,
Roll Up Your Sleeves!

- Check the picture, and think, "What would make sense?"
- Use what's happening in the story.
- Look through the WHOLE word, part by part.
- Look for a word inside a word.
- Don't give up! Try something! Take a guess!
- **Reread and ask, "Does that sound right?"**
- **Use vowel teams, and ask, "Would a different sound help?"**

Reread and ask, "Does that sound right?"

Soon Katie began to shiver.

Use vowel teams, and ask, "Would a different sound help?"

Is it like head? ? Or is it like beach?

"Off you go. And remember that when you see a vowel team, you can think, 'Hey, I know you, you tricky vowels—and you're *not* going to trick me!'"

Word Work during Reading Workshop

WHILE KIDS ARE READING INDEPENDENTLY during today's workshop, you may want to research the room at the start of the workshop, before settling down into one-to-one conferring or pulling small groups. Go around and check each table to see what is happening. Check to make sure every student has a baggie full of just-right books and hasn't somehow wound up with books that are too easy or too hard. Check on engagement, remind kids about the Post-its they all have in their baggies, and remind them to gather ideas to talk about with their partners. A quick round of reminders about past minilessons will help kids continue to use all the strategies you've been teaching.

Throughout this bend, you've been gathering groups for small-group strategy lessons as well as guided reading. It may be the case that some of your students really need support with word work to use the strategies you've been teaching. For example, some students may not automatically recognize spelling patterns, such as consonant blends and digraphs, vowel teams, or common word endings. This will make it difficult if not impossible to use the strategy of breaking a word into parts in an effective way. Most of the intense word work will need to happen during phonics/word work time, outside reading workshop. But bringing a bit of word work into reading workshop may help some kids transfer what they've been studying in isolation during word study to the real work of reading books in reading workshop.

For example, you may have a group of students who have been studying closed and open syllables during word study time. During reading, you might gather them together and say, "Readers—writers—let's set up our white boards to do some word work just like we do during word study time! At the top of your board, will you please write CVVC and CVV? We know that some vowels go together in words to make one sound, usually the sound of the name of the first vowel, though not always. These vowel teams can be in the middle of words or syllables that end with a consonant, like the word *train*, which we know is a closed syllable. Go ahead and write *train* under CVVC. But in other words or syllables with vowel teams, the vowel team comes at the end of the word, like in the word *tray*, which is an open syllable. Now write *tray* under CVV. When

you read, you have to keep in mind that there are lots of vowel teams that make a long vowel sound and that they can come at the beginning, middle, or end of a syllable. Let's warm up on white boards by sorting words as we write them."

You could then read students a list of words, such as *rain*, *trail*, and *stray*. As you read the list, coach kids to write the words in the appropriate columns. Point out that the long *a* sound is spelled one way in the closed syllable words, and another way in the open syllable words. When in the middle of a syllable (closed syllable), it is spelled *ai*.

You can then show kids how this transfers to reading. As you refocus the students to hunt in their books for these patterns, remind them, "There's a tricky thing about vowel teams, though. They don't always make the sound of the first vowel, so remember, keep an eye out for those tricky vowel teams and try out more than one sound to figure out a word that makes sense for the story."

MID-WORKSHOP TEACHING   Not Forgetting the Story!

"Readers, sometimes when you focus too much on solving hard words, you forget to think about the content of what you are reading. Right now, will you pause in your reading and see if you can remember the way the book you are reading goes. Just try to recall what the book says without even looking back." I gave them a minute to do that and then said, "Go back to the start of the book and just leaf through the pages, looking at the pictures and reading a few words, and try to let that work make you remember even more of the book." As children worked, I coached a few to do this with a previous book as well. "I know all you want to do is keep on reading. You can do that. But remember, thinking about words is only one important part of reading. Thinking about the story in your book is equally important."

Playing Guess the Covered Word with a Partner

Continue the work of word solving by playing a partner game.

"Readers, it is just about time to get together with your partner, but before you do, I want to teach you that you can play a fun game! In our lesson today, I covered a few words in *Katie Woo Has the Flu* so that we could figure them out together. I know you played this game often in first grade, too! It's called Guess the Covered Word. Well, you can do that same work with your partner! I put some small Post-its on your tables. Go ahead and cover up a few words in your book. Then, when you read with your partner, you can play the game together. Remember to coach your partner to use more than one strategy to figure out a word!"

FIG. 10–4   A book marked up to play "Guess the Covered Word"

Session 11

Readers Have Strategies for Figuring Out Brand-New Words, Too

MINILESSON

CONNECTION

Celebrate children's word-solving resolve. Point out that second-graders encounter words they can say but still don't understand. In those instances, the book is teaching them vocabulary.

"Readers, guess what? I don't see any 'help me, help me' readers in this room! Instead I see 'roll up your sleeves and solve the problem' people! You've got what it takes to tackle trouble, and that means you are really growing! How many of you know a handful of strategies for figuring out tricky words?" Thumbs went up and I nodded.

"You are good at figuring out words like this," and I wrote *rattlesnake* on the board. "You chunk the word into parts, you read it part by part, you think, 'Have I heard that before?' and pretty soon a rattlesnake is right there in the front of your mind, rattling its tail at you.

"But there's *another* kind of word that's tricky, and this is a kind of word that kids start seeing in second grade. These are words that aren't too tricky to say, but even after you say the word, you still think, 'Huh?' The meaning of the word is the tricky part.

"When you are reading along and you bump into a word that you can *say*, but you don't know what it *means*, your book is teaching you new vocabulary, if you let it."

❖ **Name the teaching point.**

"Today I want to teach you that readers understand that easy words aren't always as easy as they seem. Once readers figure out how to *say* a word, they know to stop and think, 'Wait, but what does this word mean in this story?'"

IN THIS SESSION, you'll teach children that there are other words—new vocabulary words—that might trick them, and when readers come to a tricky word they don't know, they think about what that word means in the story.

GETTING READY

✔ Prepare a short sample of writing that includes a vocabulary word that your children likely have never heard or seen in print (see Teaching and Active Engagement).

✔ Ask students to bring two Post-it notes and a writing utensil with them to the rug (see Teaching).

✔ Choose a page or two from *Katie Woo Has the Flu*, or whatever demonstration text you are using for this bend, to model the work of determining the meaning of vocabulary words (see Teaching).

✔ Prepare a sentence strip containing a sentence with a made-up word and highlight the made-up word (see Active Engagement).

✔ Display the anchor chart "When Words Are Tricky, Roll Up Your Sleeves!" and have the strategy "Don't just SAY the words, figure out what they MEAN too!" close by, ready to add to the chart (see Link).

TEACHING

Introduce the fact that a familiar word can have more than one meaning. Suggest that when the usual meaning doesn't make sense, readers need to work toward a new understanding of the word.

"Let me show you what I mean. Here is a word that I think you can probably say and pronounce, but I am not sure that you all know what it means."

I wrote the word *fixing* on the white board. Kids smirked and giggled a bit. "I know that word!" called out one student. "Do you? Right now, on one of your Post-its, make a little sketch that shows what you think it means." Kids got busy. Most sketches showed people making repairs to cars, bikes, or toys.

"Ah! Yes, this word sometimes does mean to repair things. You fix things after they are broken. But this is a *tricky* word. Read this sentence, and think to yourself, 'What does it mean in *this* story?'"

I showed kids the sentence, written on a white board.

> "What are we fixing for lunch today?" asked Lily.

"*Now* what does this word mean? When you read 'fixing for lunch,' what did you picture? Make a new sketch that matches the story."

Show a second example, and then recruit the kids to join you in thinking through a synonym that could replace the troublesome word.

"Here's one more example, from *Katie Woo Has the Flu*. When I get to the highlighted word, think along with me, what does this word *really* mean within this story? I'll give you a hint: the highlighted word doesn't just mean 'medicine' like you might think."

> Katie's mom gave her
>
> pills to take. "Yuck," Katie
>
> groaned. "Pills are such . . .
>
> <u>pills</u>."

This lesson signals a momentous shift in reading development. For most J and above readers, word solving is more about understanding words than decoding them. This is teaching that will carry across the second-grade year.

The word fixing is a word that many children will be able to define easily, but its meaning may be confusing as used in the example provided. You might choose to give a few of these examples for added practice and fun.

FIG. 11–1   Sage draws her definition of the word *fixing* before and after she hears the word in context.

"When I first read that, I went, 'Huh? That doesn't make sense! Why would it say that pills are pills?' Whenever I say 'Huh?' to myself, I know I need to stop and think about it a little more. Katie groans, and she doesn't want to take the medicine. What do you think? Talk with each other."

I gave the children time to talk and then said, "One strategy I use is to cover up the hard word, and replace it with a word that really makes sense. Try that with me. Then the story would say, 'Pills are such . . . What?' The kids called out, "Bad things," "Annoying things," and I nodded, repeating their suggestions within the sentence. "So we're thinking that in this story, the word *pill* also means something that is annoying or unpleasant, right?" Then I added, "Did you see that when a word didn't make sense, we took the time to puzzle through what it might mean in this sentence?"

ACTIVE ENGAGEMENT

Turn the work over to kids. Remind them of the two strategies they've just witnessed—picturing the meaning of the sentence and substituting synonyms.

"Now, can you try this on your own? You just used two strategies for figuring out the meaning of words: one, picturing the story in your mind and thinking of a word that makes sense and, two, covering up the tricky word and thinking of another word or words that could replace it.

"These are strategies that you already use all the time when you come to words you've never seen, but you can also use these strategies anytime you find yourself saying, 'Huh? What?' or 'That's strange. That didn't really make sense!'

"Will you read this sentence and figure out what the highlighted word means? This time I know it will be a new word for all of you, because guess what? I made it up!" I taped the sentence strip to the board.

> Beautiful white snow **foofled** the entire playground. The kids couldn't wait to put on their snow-
> suits and jump in it.

"Don't say it. First, just think. Make a picture in your mind. Picture snow, a playground, the kids can't wait to jump in the snow. Now pretend to cover the word with your finger. What other words would make sense there? Turn and tell your partner what you think my made-up word, *foofled*, must mean in this story."

"I heard some of you say the word *covered*. That would make sense here!"

A made-up word guarantees that none of your kids will already know the word. Also, it highlights strategies for figuring out any word! You might choose to practice this with real words as well. Try sentences like these: "Don't bug me!" Or "There was a spray of flowers at the front of the lawn." Or "She wore a jumper over her shirt to keep her warm."

LINK

Remind children of their growing list of strategies for getting themselves unstuck as readers.

"Remember how I compared you to Jack's beanstalk at the beginning of this unit? How I said that like that beanstalk, each of you would grow and grow and grow as a reader? Today I saw that stretching. Not only did you apply the strategy I taught, but you also drew on all that you knew from before today to figure out a word you'd never seen or heard before!

"You know what else is growing like Jack's beanstalk? Your list of word-solving strategies! Look here, on the chart. Let's add today's strategy."

Supporting Vocabulary

THIS WOULD BE A GREAT TIME to pull a few strategy groups to support different levels of vocabulary development. One of these groups might reinforce the teaching in the minilesson, helping children who seem to read right through words without thinking about their new meanings. For this group, it will be helpful to look through the students' books *before* you gather. Leave Post-its on pages where you think the children are missing the intended meaning of words. Then begin your teaching by saying, "Readers, you'll notice that a few of your books have some extra Post-its in them."

Let the children look through their baggies to find the books you have marked up. "In each of those books, on each page that I have marked, there are words that have confusing meanings. Just like we noticed in our minilesson that the word *pill* meant something new in the Katie Woo book, there are words in your books that have another, new meaning. Right now I would like you to read the books that I marked up and, when you get to a page with a Post-it, slow down, look for a word that might mean something new, and sketch what you think it means on your Post-it!" For this lesson you will not need to do any demonstration, because recalling the minilesson will be enough. Instead, spend the balance of time in your small group coaching the children as they read to figure out the meanings of words.

With another group of students, you might choose to teach children that just as words can have other, new meanings, so can phrases or sayings. You might start this group by pointing out how much trouble Amelia Bedelia confronts when she does not understand phrases like "dress the turkey" or "draw the drapes." Let the children know that they need to be on the lookout for sayings in their books, because often they can be the reason readers get confused. Teach them that just as we can substitute a familiar word for a new word to help us understand, we can do the same with a saying. Of course, you will want to coach the children as they practice this work. You may decide to hand them each a book that is full of such sayings, such as an Amelia Bedelia book if the level is appropriate. Otherwise, coach the children in their own books, helping them to stop and substitute when needed.

Of course, some of your children will need support with what to do when they read a word they have never seen before. You will want to teach the children that in the moment of reading, it is often best to make your best guess at a meaning and keep

(continues)

(continues)

MID-WORKSHOP TEACHING
Noticing When a New Word Has Two Smaller Ones in It

"Readers, eyes up here a second. I was just peeking over Caleb's shoulder, and I saw him do something that the rest of you may want to try. Caleb was trying to figure out a particularly long word that he didn't recognize. First, he put the letters together and pronounced the word, but he still didn't know it. Then, Caleb discovered something! When he chunked the word, it formed two smaller words he *did* know! This is the word." I turned and wrote it on chart paper:

extraordinary

"Thumbs up when you see the two smaller words in this long word!"

When many thumbs were up, I asked for kids to help, and they soon established that the word contained *extra* and *ordinary*. Nodding, I added, "Like Caleb, I bet you know what each of these words means. *Extra* means . . . ?" The class pitched in, and it was established that *extraordinary* means "better than ordinary."

"Brand-new, long words won't always break down into two smaller words, but sometimes they do. And when that happens, you can ask yourself, 'What does each of these two words mean, and what do I get when I put them together?'"

going. This might require rereading a chunk of text in search of clues or reading ahead a bit to figure out a new word—just like they do when word solving. You might also model how to use a Post-it to mark these confusing words so that children can go back later to discuss the meaning of the word with a partner, teacher, or parent.

Each of these small-group topics will be useful to children periodically through the year. Starting the year off by encouraging children to talk about words and their meanings will give children a number of strategies they can use and multiply the number of ways partners can help each other.

Noticing When Tricky Words Make Writing Powerful

Invite children to find places where their tricky words actually added to the sound and craft of the text, and then conduct an symphony share.

"Well, I'm wondering if some of the tricky words you found in your book might be words your author chose to make the writing powerful, to be more precise and specific. Will you take a minute to look back over your books to find places where the tricky words—once you figured them out—really added to the book? When you've found a line in your book, put up a thumb and we will do another symphony share, so that we can all enjoy these fabulous new words!"

Just a minute or two later, I lifted my pretend baton and pointed to children one by one to read a line from their books.

FIG. 11–2   A Juicy Words chart is a great place to collect new vocabulary.

Readers Check Themselves and Their Reading

IN THIS SESSION, you'll teach children that readers use strategies to check themselves and fix their mistakes as they read.

GETTING READY

✔ Give Partner 1s one set of jokes, written on a scrap of paper, and give Partner 2s another set so that partners each have different jokes (see Teaching and Active Engagement).

✔ Prepare a second set of jokes for partnerships, as above (see Teaching and Active Engagement).

✔ Prepare a one-day chart titled "Readers Check Themselves" (see Teaching and Active Engagement).

MINILESSON

CONNECTION

Share the story of telling a joke that backfired because you misread the punch line.

"I just got a new joke book. I love joke books, and I *love* making my brother laugh, so I called him up last night to read him some of the jokes. I read one joke and then another and another, and soon he was laughing so hard he could hardly breathe. But, I read him one more joke. Do you want to hear it?"

> *Question: How do you know when it's raining cats and dogs?*
>
> *Answer: When you step into a* puddle!

The class tried to laugh but mostly looked at each other confused. I didn't leave them to wonder for long. "Not that funny, right? You all reacted just like my brother did—except, then he added, 'Are you sure you read that right?' I looked back at the book and tried again":

> *Question: How do you know when it's raining cats and dogs?*
>
> *Answer: When you step into a* poodle!

The class sighed with understanding, and a few children let out genuine chuckles this time.

"We all know that making mistakes when we read happens—right? And we all know that mistakes in reading can make a book or a joke make no sense at all—right? But here's the thing I realized last night. When my brother caught my mistake, I didn't get to make him laugh. If I had caught it *myself*, I could have quickly fixed it and gotten a chuckle out of him after all."

Name the teaching point.

"Today I want to teach you that readers don't wait for someone else to catch their mistakes. They don't wait for someone else to check them. Instead, they check *themselves*. They stop as soon as something doesn't seem right and fix it up."

The connection requires that you ham it up a bit. Be sure your readers understand that you wanted the joke to be funny, but then you misread and it all fell apart.

TEACHING AND ACTIVE ENGAGEMENT

Invite children to read jokes to each other, practicing first so that they can fix their own mistakes and get the laugh.

"Readers, I thought we could have some fun fixing our own mistakes and telling jokes, too! Here's how it will work. I am going to hand out some jokes written on little strips of paper. You will have a minute to read these jokes to yourself and fix up any mistakes. Each partner will get different jokes. Now remember, jokes are tricky. To make them funny, you need to read them just the way they are written. Partner 2 will read the jokes to Partner 1 first, and Partner 2, if you read them correctly, you just might get a laugh! Then you'll switch. Ready?"

Hand out jokes with puns and plays on words for kids to tell each other.

I handed out the jokes, many of which had puns like the poodle joke. I listened in as kids read the jokes to themselves, but I held back, trying not to alert them when they made mistakes. I also warmed kids up, laughing a bit at all the jokes as I read over their shoulders. Then I announced, "Okay, Partner 2, are you ready? Go!" Children told jokes and chuckled, hamming it up and reading the jokes multiple times to the kids around them. Then I gave Partner 1 the signal to read.

Second-graders are still learning to understand jokes, so ones that are simple plays on words usually go over best. Complicated riddles and long jokes, on the other hand, will pull the focus away from the reading work, so you'll want to avoid those.

Engage kids in another round of joke telling, but this time ask them to research how they fix their mistakes.

"Did all your jokes work?" The class cheered. "Great! Then we are ready for a new round, but this time while you get ready to tell your jokes, I want you to be researchers. I want you to research *how* you fix up your mistakes when you do it all on your own. We will share out our strategies *before* we read our jokes. Ready? Read and *research*!" I quickly handed out new jokes to everyone while watching and listening to them prepare.

Chart what students notice about how readers check themselves.

Again I circulated, looking for readers who were checking themselves. Often I could tell kids were checking by the way they pointed to just one word on the paper or when their eyes became fixed. I shook hands and high-fived kids as they fixed their mistakes on their own, and then prompted them to think about how they did it. "Readers, before you read your jokes to your partner, take a minute to share how you fixed up your mistakes." Partners shared, clutching their jokes so they wouldn't be revealed, I jotted a list of what I heard (adding anything else I wanted them to notice).

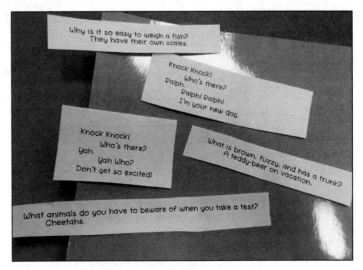

FIG. 12–1   Jokes to engage and challenge your readers

When I reconvened the group, I said, "Wow, what great researchers! You noticed so many things you did to catch your own mistakes! Did you think of the same things that I thought of?" I asked as I pointed to and read the one-day chart I had prepared.

Readers Check Themselves

- Stop when it doesn't sound right.
- Don't give up.
- Use different strategies.
- Make it make sense.
- Reread.

Again, give readers the chance to read their jokes and have a laugh.

"Okay, readers, Partner 1 will go first this time. Read your jokes!" I laughed along as all Partner 1s read their jokes, sometimes coaching them to explain why they were funny. Then I called the class back to order. "Readers, that was a lot of fun, *and* it was a great way to start the very grown-up work of fixing your own mistakes!"

LINK

Encourage readers to make an "I'll Fix My Own Mistakes" pledge.

"Readers, when grown-ups want to seal a promise, they often make a pledge. Since you are becoming such grown-up readers, I think it is time for you to make a pledge to fix your own mistakes. Are you ready?" I waited for nods, then put my left hand on my heart and raised my right hand, encouraging the children to do the same. "Okay, repeat after me: 'I do solemnly promise to fix my *own* mistakes when I read.'" The children repeated my pledge with some seriousness and then giggles.

"Remember, second-grade readers, you made this pledge, so from now on, as soon as something doesn't seem right, stop and fix it up!"

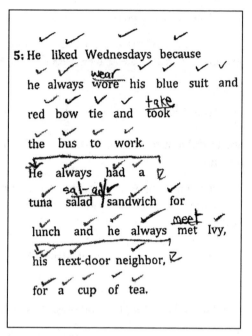

FIG. 12–2 When children don't fix their own mistakes, reading comprehension falters. Be on the lookout for readers like this one, who sail past their miscues.

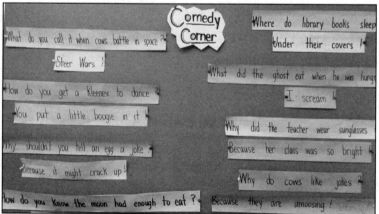

FIG. 12–3 This "Comedy Corner" bulletin board is a fun way to collect jokes in the classroom.

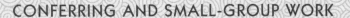

Self-Monitoring while Reading

AS YOU CONFER TODAY, you'll want to be on the lookout for any children who aren't successfully self-monitoring as they read. Maybe they were able to do so during the minilesson itself, but now, when reading on their own, they are skipping right by mistakes, not stopping to correct them. First, spend a moment to check that the level of books these readers are holding is truly just right. If the level seems right, convene a group of these readers. You might start by saying, "I gathered you together because you all are still running right over your mistakes. Here's the thing, readers. If you don't read the exact words on the page, you'll either miss out on some of the great parts *or* you'll stop understanding the story, and remember, if you're not understanding, you're not really reading at all!" This may sound a little blunt, but it is incredibly important not only to teach kids the skills and strategies they need but to tell them *why* your teaching matters. For this lesson, children will need to have a fresh text to read that is a little on the tricky side. After all, you want the children to make mistakes so that they can fix them.

If your group is composed of children who are mostly at the same level, you can start this group with one shared text. Conduct the first part of the lesson as a shared reading. You might choose to point to the words but stay quiet so that the children can really hear themselves when they make a mistake. Each time they do, give the children a knowing glance that says, "Fix it!" or tap the "When Words Are Tricky, Roll Up Your Sleeves" chart. After just a few pages, hand every other child a copy of the book and let them continue their reading with a partner. Invite one partner to read, and ask the other partner to simply tap the reader when a mistake is made. This lightens the scaffold, and though the reader will still be depending on someone else to notice her mistakes, she'll become increasingly aware of what mistakes feel like as she reads. Finally, hand out a copy to all of the readers and let the children finish the book independently. Now you can listen in, looking for the self-monitoring to kick in.

If your group of students is not made up of one level of readers, you can go straight to the partnership work. Again, after explaining your reason for calling the group together, hand out one text for each partnership. Watch as these readers coach each other. Noticing a partner's mistake will strengthen a reader's ability to notice her own mistakes, too. When partners say too much, remind them that their job is to point out the error, not fix it. Once each child has had a chance to coach and to be coached, move the readers back into their independent books. Listen in and watch as they catch their own errors.

MID-WORKSHOP TEACHING
Setting a Balanced Reading Pace

"Readers, eyes up here quickly. I just realized that I've been giving you mixed messages. *Sometimes* I tell you to read more books, more words, faster, faster, faster! And *other times* I tell you to slow down, to pause your reading when you come to a tricky word.

"The thing is, reading is a balancing act. You're in second grade now, and you're in charge of your own reading, which means you need to find a reading pace that allows you to do *both* things. On the one hand, you want to push yourself to read as much as possible. But on the other hand, you don't want to race through your books so quickly that you don't catch your own mistakes. So as you keep reading today, set the best pace for yourself. And know that your pace will likely change—often in the middle of a single reading session, even—depending on what you encounter in your books."

Discussing Fix-Up Strategies

Check in with children about what they did to self-correct as they read today. Remind them that partners can learn from listening to each other's strategies for fixing mistakes.

"Readers, hands up if you fixed any of your own mistakes today." Most raised their hands. "Before you read with your partner today, briefly tell the story of one mistake you fixed. How did you know to stop? What did you do next—how did you fix your mistake? What did you do after you fixed your mistake? As you listen to your partner, think about what you might learn from him or her. Did your partner do something you might try the next time you come to a tricky part?"

Congratulate readers on their growth and give them a chance to celebrate.

"Wow, readers! In just a few weeks of second grade, you have grown *so much*, just like Jack's beanstalk! You have learned that readers don't just read books; they choose *how* to read those books! Give yourselves a round of applause for all your practice in choosing how you read!" I smiled as the children cheered themselves.

"But that's not all! You have also learned that readers don't wait around for other people to help them read, or for other people to *fix* their reading. No! You guys roll up your sleeves and do *all* of it, *all on your own*. Give yourselves another round of applause!"

Authors Have Intentions

IN THIS SESSION, you'll teach children that readers pay attention to author's craft not only when they write but also when they read, noticing what authors do, why they do it, and how.

GETTING READY

✔ Prepare a read-aloud to model stopping to react to the text. We suggest *Those Darn Squirrels* (see Teaching).

✔ Gather Post-its to use to model stopping and jotting (see Teaching).

✔ Ask students to bring their book baggies, Post-it notes, and a writing utensil to the rug (see Active Engagement).

✔ Prepare a new chart for the bend, titled "Authors Have Intentions—So Pay Attention!" and be ready to add the strategy—"NOTICE, STOP, and THINK: WHAT part is powerful? WHY is it powerful? HOW did the author do it?" (see Link).

✔ Create a new one-day chart called "Learning Writing Moves from Our Favorite Authors." The version of the chart used in the Units of Study in Opinion, Information, and Narrative Writing is included in the online resources (see Share).

✔ Ask students to bring the books they marked, noting authors' craft (see Share).

MINILESSON

CONNECTION

Announce that starting today, children will apply what they are learning as writers to their work as readers to grow that work. They will read like writers.

"Readers, have you noticed that you've been growing like beanstalks every day, not *just* as readers, but as *writers*, too? Well, guess what? You are now ready to take what you've learned in writing to grow your reading! It's almost like you can climb our beanstalk into writing workshop, collect all you've learned there, and bring it back down to reading workshop to help you read and think in new ways! But for this new growth to happen, you need to start reading like writers—not just when we read books during writing workshop—but when you read *any* book, *any* time."

Remind children that authors write powerfully—whether they are writing something serious, silly, or scary—with the intention to make readers react in a big way.

"Can you think of a time when you read something that made you gasp or laugh or react in some way? Masterful, powerful writing gets readers to gasp or cry or laugh or sigh. In fact, any time you have a reaction in your *reading*, that is a sign of some powerful *writing*, because your reactions are part of the author's plan."

❖ **Name the teaching point.**

"Today I want to teach you that readers notice the ways authors make them *react* when they read. When readers chuckle or sigh or whimper or gasp, they *stop*. Then they reread and think, '*Why* did the author do that?' and '*How* did the author do it?'"

TEACHING

Invite children to help you select a part of the read-aloud text that got them to react in a big way.

"Readers, let's try this out together with our read-aloud book, *Those Darn Squirrels*. We have already thought a lot about this book as readers. Now let's read it as *writers*.

"Think again back to when you were reading and you reacted to a part, maybe by laughing or feeling scared or curious. That part was really powerful, wasn't it? Today we are going to look in *Those Darn Squirrels* for a powerful part—that is, *any* part that got us to react in a big way. Then we'll think through *why* we reacted that way and *how* the author got us to respond like that.

"When you see a part that made us chuckle or sigh or whimper or gasp, will you put up a big *stop* sign with your hand?" I flipped through a few pages of the book and then lingered at the first reaction Post-it. Many children took the hint and put up a *stop* hand.

"That's right! When we read this page we had a *big* reaction, and we decided to leave a Post-it here as a reminder."

Demonstrate how you stop to notice and name the author's craft technique. Then jot the author's techniques on a Post-it to use later.

"So, now, let's ask ourselves those two questions. First, *why* did we react to this? *Why* is it powerful? Because it was funny, right? This part made us laugh out loud!" I quickly reread just a line or two from the text that caused the reaction.

> *Old Man Fookwire was so old that when he sneezed, dust came out. He was also a grump. He hated pie. He hated puppies.*

The kids laughed again.

"Okay, so now we need to ask the second question. We need to figure out *how* he does that! *How* does the author, Adam Rubin, make us laugh?" I reread the text again and glanced at the children, giving them time to think of their own answers.

Then I said, "Let's see, right here," I pointed to the sentence "Old Man Fookwire was so old that when he sneezed, dust came out." "That's *really* weird—and kind of gross. I know some pretty old people and none of them sneezes dust! That's a funny way to describe someone."

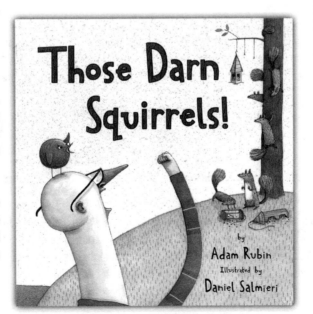

Transferring knowledge from one realm to another is paramount to growth, and so much of the craft children use as they write will help them think as they read. You might choose to point out this reading–writing connection in writing workshop this week, too.

You could decide to choose an alternative text here. Especially if many of your students are reading below benchmark, a lower-level book might be a better fit. You could choose a favorite book from a child's book baggie or another—less complex—read-aloud.

If your students are already having initial success reading like writers during writing time, you could turn this lesson into a guided inquiry. This would be a great place to hand over the reins: let the children name why the part is funny and then how the author did it. If you choose to do this, have children practice with a few pages from the read-aloud, and give less coaching through the two questions each time.

Then I pointed to "He hated pie. He hated puppies." "What a grump! Who hates pie? And who doesn't like puppies?!

"Could we say that the author made us laugh by creating a character that's ridiculous? Even his *name* is ridiculous—Old Man Fookwire! And could we also say that the author chose *surprising* details to describe Old Man Fookwire? Cool, huh? I think I'll jot that on a Post-it so I remember later!" I quickly jotted on a Post-it:

- Creates a ridiculous character

- Includes surprising descriptions/details

Debrief. Name the steps you just followed.

"Wow! We really read that like writers, huh? First we found a spot where the author made us react—that was the reading work. Then we asked *why* did this give us that reaction? And then we figured out *how* the author did it!"

ACTIVE ENGAGEMENT

Invite partners to work together, reading like writers in their own books.

"Are you ready to give this a go in one of your books? Great! Partner 2, let's start with your book. Remember, you'll want to find a spot where the author makes you react! Then you'll need to ask, '*Why* did this part make me react?' And then you can work with Partner 1 to figure out *how* the author did that. Ready? Get to work!" As readers pulled out their books, I circulated, coaching children to stop at parts in their books where they saw Post-its, to choose a part that made them react, and then to read that part out loud together.

Before too long I voiced over, "Readers, now that you have found a spot where the author made you react, you can start to talk about *why* it made you react and *how* the author did it, and don't forget when you figure it out to jot it on a Post-it!" Soon I prompted Partner 1s to pull out their books, and again I circulated, listening and coaching as the children worked.

LINK

Congratulate children on their work, reiterating what they did, and introduce a new anchor chart, "Authors Have Intentions—So Pay Attention!"

"Readers—*writers*—this is so exciting! You are on your way, using what you have learned in writing to help you *read* in a whole new way. In the next bunch of days, we are going to do lots of this work. We are going to pay close attention to the authors of our books and study *what* they are doing—*how* they are writing—and *why* their books are so good that thousands and thousands of kids read them every year. Let's get started!"

Again, if you think your students are getting the hang of this quickly, lighten the scaffold. Don't bother voicing over each question as I do here. Instead, let children discuss one question after another quickly, and then move on to the next part of the book.

I revealed the new anchor chart and sent the children off.

ANCHOR CHART

Authors Have Intentions—
So Pay Attention!

- NOTICE, STOP, and THINK:
  - WHAT part is powerful?
  - WHY is it powerful?
  - HOW did the author do it?

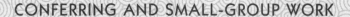

Supporting Stamina for Some and Slowing Down Speed-Reading

TEACHERS HAVE MANY GOALS at the beginning of the year. They often say, "By the end of the first unit, I want to . . . ," and then they recite a to-do list a mile long. So as you enter this last bend in the unit, you'll want to review that list quickly and find a focus that will leverage this time with your students.

One of the most important goals for the first unit is to develop stamina in your readers. Early in the unit you started tracking the class's stamina. While the bulk of your students are likely engaged throughout a lengthy workshop, others may still be struggling to keep their reading going. Resist the urge to run over to these students at the beginning of the workshop. Usually they need less support at the *beginning* of reading time. Instead, check in with those children about halfway through the reading time, just before they start to lose focus. In these check-ins, remind the children of quick strategies that will help them to stay with their work. If you have continued to have children set daily reading goals, you might ask students to study their logs and to quickly calculate how much reading they'll have to do to meet a goal. For other students, the struggle might be to simply sit still. Teach them to take a quick body break. This could include going into the hallway to do ten wall push-ups or taking a walk around the classroom before returning to reading. Teaching students how to self-manage is a major part of second grade, and during these check-ins you'll want to remind children that these are strategies that they can use on their own when they notice their focus is waning.

Most teachers also want to be sure that students are using their reading logs. This would be a good time to check around the room, glancing at reading logs, to see if they are being filled out properly and consistently. If you find that a large number of your children are not using them, this would suggest that you need to have reading set-up and clean-up routines that include filling in the logs.

If the logs are filled in, but you notice that some children are reading *way* too fast, you'll likely call a small-group strategy lesson for those children. Many advanced readers enter second grade thinking that reading is the most fun when they speed

through one book after another, never pausing to think or reflect. With this group, use the work of this bend to give them a reason to slow down. You might start the group by saying, "I was looking at your reading logs and I noticed that all of you are reading your books *super fast*. I know that sometimes it's fun to read one book after another after another, especially if you've just discovered a new series or author whom you really love. *But* there is a problem with this. When you read so quickly, you can't really appreciate the writing and what makes the books great! So today I want to teach you that when you read a great book, it helps to read a bit and then pause to think, 'What do I like here? What makes this great?' Then you can go back and reread."

Keep your coaching as light as possible. Watch your readers, and when you see them flying from page to page, give them the signal to pause and think. You might also decide to coach one child in the group toward jotting ideas on Post-its to make her thinking visible, while you coach another child to mark the parts that he's thought about and wants to talk more about later. Remember that even though you pulled students into one group, your coaching of those students does not need to be exactly the same.

> ### MID-WORKSHOP TEACHING   Finding Small Moments in Books and Noticing the Details
>
> "Readers, something super cool is happening as you read like writers today. So many of you are finding *small moments* right in the middle of your books! Just like when you write, authors use small moments to slow down the action and give readers lots and lots of details. If you find a great small moment in your book, stop! Then reread and search for all the details the author includes. That way, you will learn more about the author's craft *and* you will enjoy the book more, too!"

Finding Writing Moves That Many Authors Use

Use a one-day chart to show how readers can notice and name an author's craft.

"Readers, I want to show you a chart that can keep track of how an author creates powerful writing." I revealed a new one-day chart. "Can you see that the columns of this chart have the three questions we studied in the minilesson?" Then I reminded children of the powerful writing we had found in our read-aloud. Using the Post-it about Old Man Fookwire, we filled in the three columns by recalling our conversation about *what* the author did, *why* it was powerful, and *how* it was done.

If you have the second-grade Units of Study for Teaching Writing, *you can use the chart called "Learning Writing Moves from Our Favorite Authors," which was created for Jane Yolen's* Owl Moon.

Learning Writing Moves from Our Favorite Authors

WHAT is powerful?	WHY is it powerful?	HOW is it done?
• the description of Old Man Fookwire and his name	• makes the reader laugh	• creates a ridiculous character • includes surprising descriptions/details

Invite children to share the powerful writing from their books and add their examples to the chart.

"Now look at the Post-it you have in *your* book and tell me *what* makes the author's writing powerful, *why* the writing is powerful, and *how* the author did it." I called on several students to share out the powerful writing they had found and I recorded their information on the chart.

Once several rows were filled in, I asked, "Did any of you find some of these moves in *your* book? Is it possible that different authors use some of the same writing moves?" Most everyone nodded in agreement. "So, can we say that there are certain things that authors do to make their writing powerful and that we can try that in our own writing, too?" All heads nodded this time.

"As you continue to read your book, be sure to notice what the author does to make the writing powerful. Mark the best places with a Post-it so that we can keep the chart going and be ready to do some powerful writing!"

Learning Writing Moves from Our Favorite Authors

WHAT is powerful?	WHY is it powerful?	HOW is it done?
Page 1 of <u>Owl Moon</u>	feels like you are there	names what character exactly: • sees • hears • feels makes a comparison
Right before owl arrives in <u>Owl Moon</u>, when the father calls out to it	you wonder what will happen next, and hope things turn out a certain way	• uses actions and images that show a character hopes for something • gives clues that something might happen • stretches out the story. The big thing doesn't happen right away.
showing the big idea in <u>Owl Moon</u> (pp. 11, 13, 29)	lets the reader know what is most important	uses repetition

Readers Don't Just *Notice* Craft Moves—They *Try* Them!

IN THIS SESSION, you'll teach children that readers can try the author's craft moves in their writing, too.

GETTING READY

✔ Write the message of the teaching point ("Turn your thoughts into action!") on the white board or on chart paper (see Connection).

✔ Prepare to use and add to the shared writing piece you are using for writing workshop (see Teaching and Active Engagement).

✔ Use the class read-aloud, *Those Darn Squirrels*, or an alternative text, to model noticing and trying author's craft. Make sure some pages are marked with Post-its describing the author's craft moves that the children have noticed (see Teaching and Active Engagement).

✔ Display the anchor chart "Authors Have Intentions—So Pay Attention!" so that it is ready to refer to (see Link).

MINILESSON

CONNECTION

Ask students to set up both their reading and writing materials before joining you for the lesson.

"Writers, I mean *readers*. Wait, no, I mean writers." I chuckled at my joke, then added, "Today you will be both, so will you please set up your reading spot with both your reading materials *and* your writing materials? Then you can join me on the rug."

I moved about the room for a minute, helping students find ways to organize all their materials at their reading spots. When everyone was settled on the rug, I began the lesson.

Tell students that adults don't just think about doing something. They take action.

"Readers *and writers*, today you will 'Turn your thoughts into *action*!'" I paused to show the phrase written out on the white board. "How many of you have heard that phrase before?" A few hands went up. "This is a phrase, or a saying, that grown-ups use to motivate themselves. It means 'take what you have been thinking about doing and start actually *doing it!*'

"Yesterday, you read and noticed all different kinds of craft moves that your authors were using, right?" I indicated that the children should answer with a loud and proud, "Right!" and they did.

✤ **Name the teaching point.**

"Today I want to teach you that when readers notice an author's craft move—and they *really* love it—they take action. They try it in their *own* writing."

TEACHING AND ACTIVE ENGAGEMENT

Invite children to choose a page they love in the read-aloud text, and remind them of the craft moves the author used on that page.

"So now you know why you need both your reading and your writing materials today, right? Before you dig into your own books and your own writing, let's take action together, applying something we admire in our read-aloud, *Those Darn Squirrels*, to the book we are writing together about our class pet, Goldie." I propped up both our read-aloud and our writing on the easel ledge.

"So we will need to start by finding a part that we *really* love in *Those Darn Squirrels*. Give me a stop hand when I get to a part with an author's craft move that you want to try." I opened the book and paged through it slowly. A few hands rose for one part or another, but I kept going, waiting for a page that generated a stronger reaction. The moment I turned to page 16, a whole class's worth of stop hands shot up.

FIG. 14–1 Reading spots set up with both reading and writing materials

"Wow! So many of you agree that this is a part you really love. Let's check to see if we already jotted how the author used craft on this page." I pointed to the Post-it and read it out loud: 'The character talks and sounds *real*.' Oh, right. This is the part when the squirrels just ate all the bird food, remember? We all agreed that we could really hear the birds' voices yelling at the squirrels and Old Man Fookwire's voice yelling, and we could picture those squirrels just lying back, saying, 'Yum!' The author *intentionally* chose the words to sound like each of the characters—right? This is a really masterful part! So we are done, right?"

I played as if I were cleaning up the materials, until the children yelled, "No!"

Shift from finding craft moves to trying them out in a shared writing piece, inviting children to do this with you.

"Oh, right, we need to *take action!* Okay, let's turn our attention to our writing. We need to find a place where we can try making our characters talk, but they won't say just *anything*, right? We want them to sound *real*, just like Fookwire and the birds and the squirrels do." I read the class story slowly so children could think about where to try our new craft move.

> *"Tenzing, time to feed the fish!" Elizabeth said.*
>
> *We heard Tenzing crying. We all went to the fish tank. The room was filled with silence, just like before a storm. No one spoke. All of the children were huddled around the bowl, shoulder to shoulder. We could barely hear each other breathe.*

The class book about Goldie is developed in Lessons from the Masters, *the parallel second-grade unit in writing from the series* Units of Study in Opinion, Information, and Narrative Writing. *Obviously, you'll use your own class story from your writing workshop here.*

Using the same piece of writing that you are developing in writing workshop solidifies the reading–writing connections you aim for children to make during this bend. It also provides an additional scaffold, because it gives students a chance to try out the craft work together in the same piece of writing.

We saw our Goldie, floating on top of the water. She wasn't swimming. She was belly up in the tank. Her eyes were blank. They stared at nothing.

"What should we do?" Mallika said.

We looked at each other and waited and waited.

We whispered goodbye to Goldie. She didn't move. We were quiet like the night.

"Readers, *writers*, take a moment to discuss with your partner *where* in our story we might try out this craft move." As children burst into conversation, I circled the room, listening in to a few partnerships, coaching them to think about where this work would make sense. Then I quickly called the class back together.

"It seems like many of you are thinking that we could revise the first part when Elizabeth reminds Tenzing to feed the fish. Others of you are thinking we could add to the part where Malika says, 'What should we do?' Let's try both, starting at the beginning. Remember, we are trying to make the characters sound *real*, so think for a moment about exactly *how* Elizabeth would say that. Talk to your partner again."

I listened in as partnerships talked and then shared out some especially effective suggestions. We revised both parts of the class writing, trying out a few choices, before I called the lesson to a close.

LINK

Tell children that they will have two jobs today—one as a reader, and one as a writer—and name these.

"Today you will have two jobs, and you will need to take action in *both*. I'm sure that you will want to continue reading your books, admiring the author's craft moves and marking those. That will be your *reading* work." I tapped the anchor chart, "Authors Have Intentions—So Pay Attention!" "But you will also want to take action as *writers*, so when you notice something that you really love that you think will work well in your story, go ahead and try it right then and there. Off you go!"

FIG. 14–2 Keep revision strips on hand so that children can add the new craft to their writing.

Checking in on Partnerships

MOST TEACHERS put shoring up the fundamentals of partner work high on their list of goals for the first unit of study. So as students go off to read today, you might settle your focus on how well children are preparing for their partner conversations. Start by doing a quick scan of the room, stopping at tables, and looking for signs that students are readying themselves to share with others. Post-its that peek out of the edges of a book are a good indicator that children are thinking about upcoming conversations. You might also stop at a table and ask students to tell you their plans for partner time. Since today they are reading *and* writing, it will be interesting to note what students are most excited to show their partners.

If you find a few readers who are not getting ready for talk, research a little further to find out why. This could be because the child is not comprehending. Check to see if her books are a good match or if she has somehow wound up with books outside of her independent reading level. Other children just get lost in their books and forget to jot. You might suggest that these children place a Post-it every so many pages (or at the end of each chapter) as a prompt to remind them to think back over their reading for a place to share and reflect.

This might also be a good time to introduce same-book partnerships. Students who are reading at levels K and higher often start to lose focus during partner time, because their more complicated books are harder to talk about when their partner doesn't know the story. You might pull together a group of these students and tell them that once readers get into longer books, they often choose to read those books *together*. Explain that this means they shop for a book they both want to read, and they both read it. Then during partner time they can share their ideas, reactions, and excitement without having to explain every little detail of the book—because they both know it! Many teachers even choose to add a "Twin Bin" to their library for each level above

J. So, for example, the K Twin Bin will contain level K books that have been banded together in sets of two. This way the partnership can find a title and each have a copy to read.

After introducing kids to the concept of a same-book partnership, invite them to choose a book together. Once they have decided, encourage them to think about one way that they will prepare for their conversation today. Since this bend is all about noticing what the author does, this would be a good focus for their conversations. Next, encourage the children to get started. Stick around for the first minutes of their reading to be sure they are marking up their texts, before you move on the support others readers—*and writers*.

MID-WORKSHOP TEACHING   **Remembering to Write!**

"Readers, you have been reading and reading and reading for twenty-two minutes, and it seems like you could just keep going, but I am going to ask you to pause. If you haven't already, it is time to *take action as writers!* Take a moment to look through your book to find a part where your author does something you really like that you think might work well in your book, too. You can also look for ideas on the chart we made about authors' moves. If you have already made one change, try to find a second!

"Found it? Great! Now put your writing right in front of you, pick up your pen and *try it!*"

Sharing Your Action!

Celebrate students' reading stamina. Then, suggest partners share craft moves they identified in their books and how they tried those moves in their own writing.

"Readers, writing and reading at the same time made our workshop super long today. You actually worked for forty-two minutes. Give yourselves a round of applause! But now I know you really want to share all of your hard work with your partner. Right there, at your reading spot, will you get together with your partner? Share the author's craft move you admired and then show how you tried it!

"As you listen to your partner, make sure the craft move works. Give your partner a tip or a suggestion, just like you do during writing time, to help them better use the craft move!"

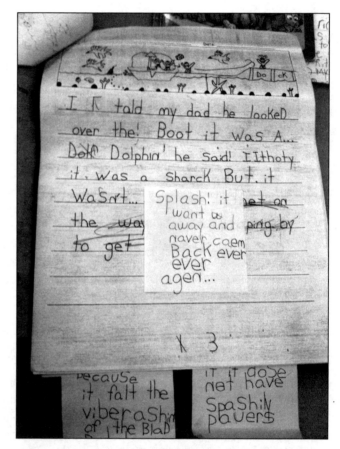

FIG. 14–3 Simone makes revisions to match the author's craft moves from her favorite independent reading book.

Session 15

Readers Think about How the Whole Book Clicks Together, Noticing Masterful Writing

MINILESSON

IN THIS SESSION, you'll teach children that readers notice the ways an author makes the parts of a story click together.

CONNECTION

Share a story about rereading a familiar text closely to notice and name the author's craft moves, emphasizing how parts of the text clicked together at the end.

"Readers, last night I was lying in bed, all cozy, rereading Mercy Watson *again*." I leaned forward and in almost a whisper admitted, "I know we have been reading it in shared reading, but I just can't get *enough of that pig*." I sat up straight again and continued, "Anyway, I had it in my head that if I read it just *one more time* I might figure out exactly what makes the writing *so* good, *so* funny, *so* masterful.

"At first I thought it was author Kate DiCamillo's way of making her readers laugh. She is so funny! And her characters sound so *real*. Even their names are specific. Eugenia Lincoln! I also noticed that Kate has a knack for stretching out the moment with tiny actions—so she pulls the reader right along with her characters, into their adventures.

"I kept reading, noticing all the craft moves Kate has carefully tucked into this one book until I reached the end. And then, I sighed a *huge* sigh because it all comes together at the end. It all makes sense. The story clicks! And that made me realize that on top of all the important craft moves readers can notice throughout a story, they have to pay particular attention to the end.

"You see, authors don't just pick words and phrases to make their writing *masterful*. They work to make *all* the parts of the story click together, especially the ending."

❖ **Name the teaching point.**

"Today I want to teach you that when readers get to the end of a story, they reread and ask, 'How does the author make the whole story click together?'"

GETTING READY

✔ Prepare to reference a familiar text, in this case a Mercy Watson book, to emphasize rereading to notice how the story fits together (see Connection).

✔ Prepare parts of the read-aloud text, *Those Darn Squirrels*, to display on the document camera or some other way and reread (see Teaching and Active Engagement).

✔ Place Post-its at rug spots for jotting, and ask children to bring a pencil with them (see Teaching and Active Engagement).

✔ Display the anchor chart "Authors Have Intentions—So Pay Attention!" and be ready to add the new strategy: "Ask, 'How did the author make this WHOLE book click together?'" (see Link).

TEACHING AND ACTIVE ENGAGEMENT

Guide children through the process of reading and recording their thinking about how the author makes the whole book fit together.

"Readers, let's practice this end-of-a-book-reflection work with our read-aloud book." I displayed *Those Darn Squirrels* on the document camera. "We've been working together to notice what Adam Rubin does to make this book so clever and funny and masterful. Today I thought we could read just the last part and think—and jot—about how the author makes the whole story click together.

"I'm going to read the end of this story to you again. As I read, listen carefully and ask yourself, 'How does the author make it all click together?' Then, when you have a thought, show me you're ready to jot by picking up the pencil and Post-its I've placed at your rug spot. That way, I'll know to pause to give you a minute to record your thinking."

Quickly retell the main events before reading aloud the first part of the ending, and channel students to jot.

Before reading, I quickly paged through the book, giving a quick retell so that the major events of the book were fresh in children's minds. Then I said, "Ready?" Children nodded and some even leaned in, excited to hear the end of the story again. I placed the book on the document camera and started to read from page 27.

> *The squirrels held a meeting deep inside a large tree. They decided to give the old man a present to make up for taking the seeds and berries.*

Before I had even finished the first sentence, many children were reaching for their Post-its, ready to jot. I finished the page and then paused, indicating that students should all jot.

Share out the main kind of thinking that children are doing, and invite them to think about what happens more than once in the story and how it is the same or different each time.

While they worked, I crouched low and moved among them, bending over kids' shoulders to see what they were writing. When I saw a child write, "The squirrels are meeting again!" I used this as an opportunity to voice over what it meant to think about the book clicking together.

"Readers, so many of you are jotting that the squirrels are doing the same sorts of things they did earlier in the book. This is one very important way to think about how a book clicks together. You can think about what is happening *again!* Right now, share with your partner what is happening again and which part that clicks with from earlier in the book."

I listened in and heard children say,

"They are making a plan again, just like the plan to get the bird food!"

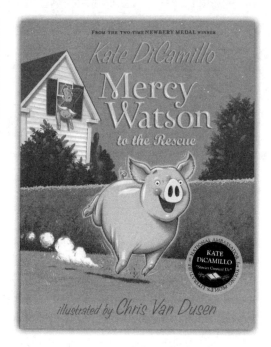

You could instead invite your readers to retell the book to each other. This would lighten the scaffold and give you a chance to assess and/or coach a few students' retells.

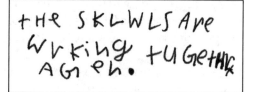

FIG. 15–1 Mario notices what is happening again and again in the story.

"They are working together."

"*But* this time they are not being mean to Mr. Fookwire. Now they are being nice!"

Remind children to think about how the *whole* book clicks together, including the beginning and the middle, as you read aloud a few more pages.

"Here you are at the end of this book, and you are pushing yourself to think about how the *whole* book clicks together, because that is a big part of what makes the writing *so* masterful! Let's read the last few pages, and this time, be sure to look for ways the *whole* book—beginning, middle, and end—click together!" I read the last few pages, and after children jotted and shared with partners, I called them together again.

Debrief. Compliment children and suggest ways they may have noticed all the parts of the book—the beginning, middle, and end—clicking together.

"Wow! So many of you are starting to notice not just how one or two parts click together, but how *all* the parts click! How many of you noticed that the squirrels work together in the beginning, and the middle, and the end?" Hands shot up in the air. "And how many of you noticed that Old Man Fookwire said, 'Those darn squirrels!' all the way through the book, even when he changed his mind and liked them at the end?" I showed a few pages on the document camera. Some children whispered that they had noticed; others showed signs of new understanding.

"This is pretty amazing, huh? You are doing even *more* thinking at the end of the book. You are noticing how the beginning, middle, and end all click together!"

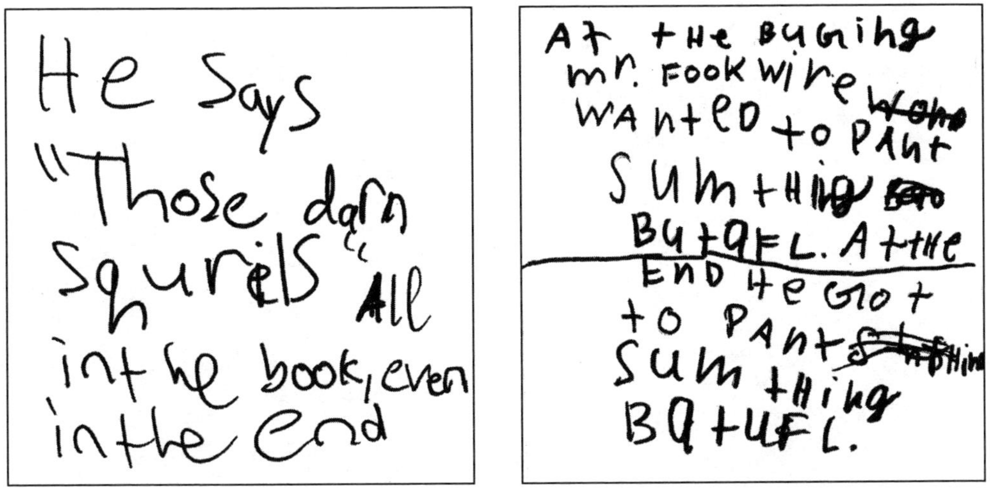

Notice that as you admire the author's craft here, you also teach children to make sense of how the ending fits with the story as a whole. Understanding how a story fits together is one of the new challenges second-grade readers will face.

FIG. 15–2   Asesha and Elan jot how the ending "clicks" with the rest of the story.

LINK

Remind children that authors work hard to make their books great in a variety of ways, and then add today's strategy to the anchor chart.

"Readers, you are becoming truly *masterful* at reading like writers! You are starting to see that authors don't just work on one word or one phrase or one part when they write. Instead, authors work to make each part of their story click with all the other parts. You might not notice this at first, but as you get to the end of your book, you'll want to be on the lookout for this masterful writing!" I displayed our chart and added to it.

ANCHOR CHART

Authors Have Intentions–
So Pay Attention!

- NOTICE, STOP, and THINK:
  - WHAT is powerful?
  - WHY is it powerful?
  - HOW did the author do it?
- **Ask, "How did the author make this WHOLE book click together?"**

Ask, "How did the author make this WHOLE book click together?"

"So, today, as you read like writers, you can notice your author's craft in each individual part, *and*, as you near the end, you can also notice how the author made the *whole* book click together! You may want to flip back through your book's pages, to notice the specific ways that the parts work together."

Assessing Retells On-the-Run and Supporting Small Groups of Readers Who Are Ready to Move Up

TODAY WOULD BE A GOOD TIME to do on-the-run assessments of your readers' ability to retell. Now that many of them are reading chapter books and lengthier picture books, their strategies for retelling will need to evolve. While level F/G readers can flip through pictures to help them retell, readers of higher-level books will end up recounting too many small details if they use this strategy. In addition, some children misunderstand what makes a strong retell, thinking that the more you tell, the better. Looking at your running record retells can help you to determine who needs some support with this important skill.

However, for students who are reading levels K and above, sometimes a running record retell is not enough. Because running records are taken from short texts, you can't always determine what a child's retell will sound like when the text is lengthier. Instead, you might ask these students to jot a retell of the last chapter book they read. Collect these and look them over quickly. Even if you don't know the book well, you will be able to determine whether the child has included the main character, what that character wants, and the main things she does to get it. The retell should also include what happened at the end. You can then use this data—and the running record data—to help you identify small groups, inform a whole-class share, or even design a minilesson, if needed.

After collecting a bit of data, you might choose to convene a small group of readers whom you think are just about ready to move up levels. These might be students who slipped from the end of last year and are growing back into their former levels or students who have simply grown because of all the reading work they've done so far this year. One way to support these readers in more challenging texts is to give them a guided reading lesson, and you might choose to do just that.

Alternatively, you might choose to give them a *level* introduction and the support of a partner as they read the first book at this new level. This might sound like, "Readers, I think you all are ready to read some new and harder books from the level *M* basket— like this Magic Tree House book. Because these books will be a stretch, I want to show

you a few things you will need to do to read them well. First, I want you to know that these books will often have two main characters, instead of one. That means you will need to make a movie in your mind that helps you see what both characters are doing. Also, in these books characters talk back and forth quite a lot. Sometimes the talking is where you find out what is happening. Pay attention to what the characters say so that you can keep track of what they are doing. One more thing that can be tricky is that when the characters talk, *sometimes* the author will tell you who is talking and *sometimes* you will have to figure it out on your own! Let me show you what I mean."

Show the children how you navigate each of these new difficulties quickly, and then turn their attention to reading with a partner. You might say, "So, readers, I'd like you to use your partner as a support as you get started with these books. I'm going to give one copy of this book to the two of you, and after you take a sneak peek, will you read the first chapter together? Your goal on this first read will be to read *all* of the words—don't let the tricky parts trip you up—*and* to figure out who the characters are and what they want. When you get to the end of the first chapter, stop and retell to each other."

(continues)

MID-WORKSHOP TEACHING
Not Waiting to Think about the Book as a Whole

"Readers, earlier I told you that you can notice how a book clicks together when you reach the end. But I want to revise that. The truth is that figuring out how a book clicks together can happen sooner than you think. You don't have to wait until the end of the book. As you read today, you can stop at the end of each part or each chapter of the book to think about how parts are linked. How do the new parts build on things the author introduces earlier?"

Stick around only long enough to be sure that the children are working well together. Then you can circulate around the room, carrying on one-to-one conferences. Return to the group in time to hear their retells. Use this opportunity to assess and coach your readers, before deciding whether you want them to reread this chapter for greater understanding or whether you think they should move on to the next. If your readers seem very comfortable in the new level, you might choose to have them read to the end of the book independently and then meet back up to discuss the book when they have finished. You will want to coach this conversation, too. Make sure that the conversation goes beyond just retelling plot points. Many strong readers just want to digest book after book without developing thoughts and ideas as they read.

FIG. 15–3 Handing out a tool like this bookmark—which reminds children of key teaching points—can support independence.

Practicing Retelling

Point out that readers need to work on their retelling skills, and demonstrate how to do this, using the read-aloud book.

"Readers, when I conferred with some of you today, I could tell that lots of you would were having a hard time retelling. Remember, when readers retell, the goal is to *quickly* tell the main things that happen in the book. It helps to do this across five fingers (even though sometimes you might need a few more fingers).

"Let me show you how I'd retell *Those Darn Squirrels* across my fingers. As I do, will you research what I do?" I began retelling the story to myself, as if the kids weren't present, putting up a finger for each plot point.

"There was a man named Old Man Fookwire who didn't like anything except birds and painting birds." I put up a finger. "Every winter the birds went south and the old man was lonely. One year Old Man Fookwire put up bird feeders to try to feed them and keep them around." I put up a second finger. "The birds loved the bird feeders—but so did the squirrels, who stole the food." I put up a third finger.

"Old Man Fookwire tried one thing after another to keep the squirrels away, and finally he succeeded, but, still, the birds left." I put up a fourth finger. "When the squirrels saw how sad he was, they tried one thing after another to cheer him up and finally, they did it! They dressed up as birds, and the old man realized he could paint them instead." I put up a fifth finger!

I looked up and said, "Turn and tell your partner what you saw me doing!"

Name what you did while retelling that you hope all the readers do—telling just the major plot points—and ask partnerships to practice retelling their books to one another.

As children talked, I leaned in to listen. Then I shared out what they noticed: that I told the story across just five fingers, listing one plot point across each finger. Some realized that I'd left out the little details as I retold.

"Readers, see how it is was short and quick? Now, you are going to work on retelling your books. Partner 1 will start. Partner 2, listen to how your partner retells and uses his or her fingers. Help make it short and quick!"

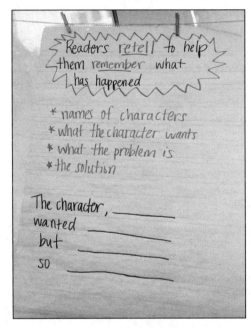

FIG. 15–4   A chart can help children remember how to keep their retells short.

Readers Think, "What Does the Author Want to Teach Me?"

IN THIS SESSION, you'll teach children that once readers have finished reading a book and know how the parts fit together, they can retell it to think about what lessons the author wants to teach.

GETTING READY

✔ Prepare to read the first few pages of a read-aloud, such as *Those Darn Squirrels* (see Teaching).

✔ Gather Post-its to model jotting while reading (see Teaching).

✔ Display the anchor chart "Authors Have Intentions—So Pay Attention!" and be ready to add the new strategy "Learn a lesson. Think, 'What does the author want to teach me?'" (see Link).

✔ Prepare chart titled "Authors Often Think Alike" (see Mid-Workshop Teaching).

✔ Choose a book with a back cover blurb and table of contents to model taking a sneak peek (see Share).

✔ Hand out a small copy of the "Readers TALK about Books" chart if you think it would be helpful for students (see Conferring and Small-Group Work).

✔ Place Post-its nearby so that children can jot lesson predictions (see Share).

MINILESSON

CONNECTION

Share a story about a time you got to see firsthand how something, in this case a ballet, was crafted. Connect this to the work children are doing studying craft.

"When I was a little girl, I went to the ballet with my grandfather. I *loved* it! I just got lost in the story of the dancing and the music. When it was over, I almost felt like I was waking up from a dream. I looked at my grandfather and said, 'It was *so* beautiful. Thank you, Grandpa!' But my grandfather explained that there was more. He knew one of the dancers, and she wanted to meet me. He led me toward the stage and then pulled the curtain back to reveal *everything*! There were people and lights and pulleys and *so* many props. In that short walk back to the dancers' dressing room, behind the curtain, I got a glimpse of how the ballet was *made*, how every part was *crafted*.

"That memory reminds me of what you all have been doing. It seems to me that you have been pulling back the curtain on your stories, too. You have been enjoying the stories and then learning about how the authors crafted those stories!"

Tell children that authors write to teach readers important lessons.

"Well, there is something else that I need to tell you. Authors don't just write to entertain us. They don't just write stories so we can say, 'Ah, nice story.' Authors often write to help us think about big ideas—to teach us important lessons."

❖ Name the teaching point.

"Today I want to teach you that once readers have finished a story and they understand how the parts click together, they know it's important to think, 'What does the author want to *teach* me?'"

TEACHING

Model retelling the first part of a read-aloud, and then invite students to take over and retell the remainder of the text to their partner.

"When I want to think about the lessons a book may be teaching, it helps to quickly retell the book, keeping in mind how the beginning, middle, and end connect. Let me show you how I do this with a book that all of us know well by now." I held up *Those Darn Squirrels* and started to retell it out loud, popping up a finger for each plot point and motioning for children to check my understanding. "So, Old Man Fookwire lives by himself outside of town. And he doesn't like anything except . . ." I left space for the children to chime in with, "Birds!"

Then I said, "You know what, you've already watched me do this. And you know this story really well. Quickly, turn and retell it to your partner!"

Invite students to think alongside you as you consider what lesson the author wants to teach you. Demonstrate making a predictable mistake, naming what the character learns.

I gave them just a minute to do this, listening in, and then said, "So, now that all the parts of the book are fresh in my mind, I need to think, 'What does the author want to *teach* me?' Hmm, . . .

"You know what? Mr. Fookwire gets grumpy a lot. That's all over the book, right? How he doesn't like *anything*." The children nodded and laughed a bit. "So, what might the author want to teach us?" I gave the students a moment to think but voiced over my own thinking as a model.

"Well, it seems like Old Man Fookwire is such a grump that he can't enjoy very much in life. He enjoys only painting and birds. Maybe the author is teaching us to . . ." I began to jot.

> Old Man Fookwire shouldn't be a grump, and he should try to like more stuff!

I displayed the Post-it note with the jot on the easel. "What do you think? Could this be the lesson that the author is trying to teach me? Wait! That's not a lesson for me. That's a lesson for Old Man Fookwire! What does the author want *me* to learn from this?" I tried again, crumpling up the first Post-it and replacing it with this one.

> Don't be a grump—give yourself a chance to like new things!

"Now that sounds like a lesson the author could teach *me*, right?"

SESSION 16: READERS THINK, "WHAT DOES THE AUTHOR WANT TO TEACH ME?"

This story could be about anything really—looking at the mechanics of a clock, peeking into the kitchen of a fancy restaurant. The point is to let children know how special it is to study how things are made, how things work. Choose a story that works for you.

This dramatic pause serves multiple purposes. It makes your think-aloud feel more authentic, and it ensures that students are not just watching you do the work but are actively thinking and generating their own ideas alongside you.

ACTIVE ENGAGEMENT

Set readers up to find more lessons in the read-aloud text. Alternate between asking partners to work together and sharing out what partnerships determined.

"Are you ready to give this a go? The story is fresh in your minds now. Might the author be teaching you other lessons? Turn and discuss this with your partner!"

I listened in and then reconvened the group, "Wow! I heard a lot of ideas about lessons in this book. It seems like this author is trying to teach us more than one thing, huh? Listen to this one":

> The squirrels learn to use their brains to be nice.

"What do you think, readers? Is this a lesson for *you*?" Some kids shook their heads no, while others looked unsure.

"It's definitely a lesson in the book, but is that the lesson for *us*? Nope, it's for the squirrels. Let's try to say it a different way so that it is the lesson the author is teaching *us!* Figure it out with your partner!"

After just a few moment we had:

> Use your smarts to be kind.

LINK

Encourage readers to add today's work to their repertoire.

"Readers, wow! You have some big work ahead of you. Remember that reading like a writer will help you pay attention to the author's intentions."

I displayed the anchor chart and read it with the class.

"But authors don't write just to entertain us. They want to teach us *lessons*, too. This is *complex* work we are doing, so you might find that you want to start with books you have already read. Then you can reread and ask yourself, "What does the author want to teach me?""

I added the newest strategy to the chart.

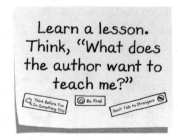

Almost every book has more than one lesson, even if some fit with the whole of the text better than others. Let your children name a variety here without sifting through for ones that are perfectly matched to the text.

ANCHOR CHART

Authors Have Intentions—So Pay Attention!

- NOTICE, STOP, and THINK:
  - WHAT did the author do?
  - WHY did the author do that?
  - HOW did the author do it?
- Ask, "How did the author make this *whole* book click together?"
- **Learn a lesson. Think, "What does the author want to teach me?"**

Supporting Readers as They Reach the End of Their Books

THE WORK OF THE LAST TWO MINILESSONS has been beefy. Helping children think and reflect at the end of their books is work that you will circle back to throughout the second-grade year. In fact, transitional readers—(the term many educators use to describe readers moving through levels J/K/L/M) need to do three major things to get a full understanding of their books. First, they need to be able to collect the important episodes in their books. This means they need to retell in meaningful chunks, rather than detail by detail, highlighting the problem and solution if the story has one. By now you have already addressed this important skill in both small-group and whole-class teaching and during reading workshop, read-aloud, and shared reading.

Second, children need to be able to make sense of the ending of the book. This is the work that you introduced to children yesterday when you taught them to figure out how the parts of their stories will fit with the ending. And, finally, children need to be able to look for the lesson and other big ideas that are embedded in the text. So, in just one unit you have started your students on the work they will practice all year long.

As you confer, make sure you are checking in on these big skills consistently. While kindergarten and first-grade teachers tend to listen to their readers read during every conference, second-grade teachers are more likely to research readers with one or more of the following questions: Who are the characters? What do they want? What are the big things that have happened so far? What happened at the end? How does that ending fit with the rest of the story? What do you think the character learned? What did the author teach you?

You will undoubtedly find students who struggle with one of these big skills at the beginning. You might choose to practice developing the skill over the course of a few days. If you wanted to help readers to work on thinking about how the ending fits with the rest of the story, your first session might center around practicing this skill in the shared reading text. You could coach children to work together and then even write out a few sentences from their discussion. For example, "At the end of *Mercy Watson*, Mercy gets buttered toast. That makes sense because at the beginning she jumped

---

MID-WORKSHOP TEACHING Making a Chart of Lessons Authors Teach in Lots of Books

"Readers, as I move around the room asking you about your authors and the lessons they are teaching, something funny is happening: it seems like there are an awful lot of lessons that sound the same—or at least similar." I paused to be sure I had everyone's attention. "For example, how many of you have a lesson in your book that is something like 'Be kind'?" I looked around the room, sometimes calling on kids who I knew had jotted something close to that to raise their hands. "Wow! That's a *lot* of authors trying to teach that same lesson." I reached over to my chart paper and started a chart.

"I bet there are a few other lessons like this one that *lots* of authors want to teach. Take a minute with your partner right now to see if you can find a few others!" I circulated among the children as they talked, calling out lessons as partnerships named them (sometimes revising them to fit more books), and then jotting them on Post-its to add to our chart. Soon our chart read like this:

Authors Often Think Alike

Lessons We Found in LOTS of Stories!
- Be Kind
- Friends Fix Lots of Problems
- Don't Talk to Strangers
- Pets Can Be Best Friends
- Think Before You Do Something Silly

"This is so interesting, isn't it? It seems like these authors sure do think a lot alike! If you are stuck, and not sure what your book is teaching you, you can always ask yourself if any of these match your book. They might! As we learn more lessons, we can always add them here."

---

out of the bed to get toast!" In the next session with this group, you might practice the same skill with a new shared text. On a subsequent day you might have partners work together to read a book and then talk about how the book fits together. In a final session, you could coach children as they read independently, helping them practice once again in their own books.

However, there will be other children who do all of this right away. When you ask questions about the ending during the minilesson, these readers roll right through them, easily answering each. You might be tempted to think, "Great! I can move on!" But this reaction would be ill advised because these skills are not static. As children read books of greater complexity, they can find new struggles with skills that used to be solidly in place. So, while your more advanced readers may have had all the answers when you taught about lessons in today's minilesson, you might find that they struggle in the longer, more complex books they are reading independently.

So if you gave a group of children a Magic Tree House book, you might want to call them together after they have finished and invite them to discuss the lessons the author includes. Prompt the children to think about the book as a whole, since in this level sometimes a character learns, for example, not to be rude in one chapter but also learns a bigger lesson that weaves through the entirety of the book. Encourage students to find evidence in their books to support their ideas and to question each other's thinking. Some teachers find that it is helpful to give these groups a small copy of the whole-class discussion chart ("Readers TALK about Books") to help them navigate these conversations.

FIG. 16–1   Giving students a small version of your whole-class discussion chart can support their talk in small groups and partnerships.

Taking a Sneak Peek to Consider an Author's Lessons Right from the Start

Explain that readers can think about lessons an author teaches before they even start reading, as they take a sneak peek.

"Readers, did you know you don't have to wait to think about the lessons an author will teach? In fact, you can make predictions about lessons when you take your sneak peek!

"Remember that when we take a sneak peek, we look at the cover, the back of the book, and the table of contents if there is one, right? Well, if you simply stop to ask, 'What might the author want to teach me?' after reading each of those parts, you'll often find the lesson before you even read!" As I spoke, I showed each part in a book that I held up to model.

Suggest readers try this work with a partner, taking a sneak peek of their books together and thinking about what the author wants to teach. Coach children to lift the level of their work.

"Try this with the help of your partner. Partner 1, pull out your book first." I waited while the children pulled out the books they had chosen to read next.

"Okay, so first look at the cover and study the picture. Think about the title. What do you think your book will be about?" I waited for a moment for the children to think and then gave them the signal to turn and talk. "Okay, readers, now that you have an idea of what the story will be about, ask yourselves, 'What might the lesson for the reader be?'" I moved about, coaching the readers. Kids who held books about friendship had little trouble predicting lessons about being kind and the importance of standing up for your friends. Other children had a slightly harder time, and I coached them but also took note so that I could form a small group to support this work.

"Readers, continue your sneak peak. Turn to the back cover and then to the table of contents. Remember, after you think about how the story will go, ask yourself, 'What might the author want to teach me about that?'" Again I circulated, coaching with questions like, "Do you still think the lesson will be . . . , or is your idea changing now?" and "That sounds like the lesson the *character* will learn. Can you think about what the lesson for the *reader* might be?" After a few minutes, I invited the children to jot their lesson predictions on a Post-it and told Partner 2 to pull out a book and do the same sneak peek work.

"Readers, you are really thinking about the lesson *before* you even read now. Wow! Tonight when you read these books at home, you can reflect on whether your predictions were correct or if the lesson turned out to be a bit different!"

FIG. 16–2   A sneak peek can help children predict both the problem AND the lesson an author will teach.

Celebrate How Much Readers Have Grown!

MINILESSON

In your connection, you will want to tell your students that today is a day for celebration. Show your students all the charts that illustrate everything they have learned this month. You might start by looking at the "Readers GROW Like Beanstalks!" chart, encouraging the children to sit up a little straighter for each strategy that they have mastered over the course of the unit. Then you might move to the "When Words Are Tricky, Roll Up Your Sleeves!" chart, inviting the children to "roll 'em up!" as you read through. Finally, direct children's eyes to the "Authors Have Intentions—So Pay Attention!" chart, perhaps asking them to lean closer and closer to the chart as you read each bullet.

You might lead into your teaching point by saying, "So far this year, I've been teaching you all kinds of things to help you grow like beanstalks, and, my goodness, you certainly have grown! I'm thinking that today, instead of me teaching you something new, you could actually share what you know with other readers. You could help other readers grow! Are you up for it?"

For the teaching point, you might say, "Today I want to teach you that when readers know a lot about a book, they can help future readers of that book really grow by leaving those readers tips, important pieces of advice. Then, when future readers pick up the book, they get a little help with their reading."

During your teaching, you can showcase a big stack of familiar books and say, "Readers, we've read each of these books together during our read-alouds and shared reading. As we read these books, we thought about how the books wanted to be read—and we made our voices match. We worked hard to read each and every word, just the way the authors wrote them. We even noticed the authors' masterful craft, and we learned the lessons they wanted to teach us. It was hard work, right?" Then, you'll want to emphasize that one way to help future readers of these books is to leave them some tips, written on Post-it notes, that will help them as they read the books themselves.

You can model picking up a book from your stack and remembering what was tricky about that book. You might say, "Oh, we loved this one, remember? But do you recall all those tricky words the author used? Sometimes we thought they meant one thing when they actually meant something else. I'm going to jot a note for future readers: 'Watch out for tricky words! They don't always mean what you think.'" Debrief the process you just went through, naming for students how you chose a familiar book, considered what was tricky about that book, and then wrote a note for future readers that told what was tricky and gave a bit of advice.

In the active engagement, turn the reins over to your readers. Hold up another familiar text from your pile, one you're certain students know inside and out, and ask them to first talk with their partner about what was tricky about that text. If their comments are vague, coach them to look back at the class charts to get ideas for what might be tricky. Highlight one or two ways the text was tricky, and then invite partners to talk about what piece of advice they would give readers to help them read this book. Students could do this work orally, writing their response in the air as you teach them to do in writing workshop, or you could distribute large Post-it notes to partnerships and have them record their responses.

In your link, emphasize that as students read today, they'll also need to take a few minutes to leave tips inside their books. This is important work, as your tone will convey to students, because the tips they leave will help future readers to grow. Also, be sure to turn your students' attention to the "Readers Read More and MORE! Growing Stamina Every Day" chart. Remind them that a big part of their reading growth this month has been about their reading stamina. You might let them know that today, as they go off to read, they'll also read to break their stamina record. Then start your reading timer, and send them off! If students jotted their tips on Post-it notes during the active engagement, invite them to stick the note on the book before heading off to read.

CONFERRING AND SMALL-GROUP WORK

In your conferring, you'll want to move about the room oohing and aahing over all your readers' tips and then help them strengthen the advice they give. "That is a tricky part. What did you do when you first read it? Write down that tip!" you might say to one reader. In addition, you'll want to study your conference notes to determine which students you'll check in with one more time before the end of this unit.

Then, too, you'll want to think ahead to the upcoming informational reading unit. Be sure to note the skills children will need and ask yourself, "Who will need support with those skills up front, right away?" Jot notes to help you form small groups right from the get-go. Also be on the lookout for kids you are just about ready to move to new levels. Make a list of these students for potential guided reading groups, so that you can start to pull books and write book introductions that will be ready for you in the first bend of the next unit.

wach out! Junnie.B. makes up a lot of silly words!

Super silly Book Make sure you get the Jokes!

FIG. 17–1   Paloma and Chase leave behind advice for the next reader.

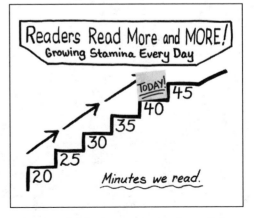

FIG. 17–2   Celebrate your readers' growth by noting how much longer they can read now.

Mid-Workshop Teaching

In your mid-workshop teaching, start to spread the feeling of celebration. You might say something like, "Readers, I'm sorry to stop you, but I just had to share some of the tips you're leaving each other. They're huge and powerful, and I know they'll help other readers grow." Then, you could highlight a few tips readers have already left in their books. Ask partners to share just one tip they've already left, and then rally them to continue reading so they break their stamina record.

SHARE

For the share, invite your readers to join you in a circle with all the books they've left tips in for a messy—and *fun*!—library reorganization party. You might say to kids, "You left such powerful tips for readers in your books today. I'm thinking that one more place you could give advice today is in our classroom library. I have a bunch of empty bins here, and I was thinking you might want to reorganize our books in some way. Maybe one bin could have books we recommend. And maybe another bin could have books readers learn valuable lessons from. And a third could have books with really tricky phrases. I'm sure you'll invent others! What do you think?" Then, you can invite kids to look at all the books in their baggies and think about how they want to organize them. In many classrooms, kids choose to make bins with different lessons on them like, "Friends who make a difference!" or "Don't give up!" Then have kids fill the bins with books that convey those messages. Lots of books will end up back in the bins they came from, but others will likely find new homes in new bins or on display shelves with signs that help others know why they are so special.

FIG. 17–3 Children can help to reorganize the library—writing their own labels—so that some bin titles reflect their recommendations and new thinking about lessons.

Read-Aloud

GETTING READY

Session 1

✔ Choose a picture book with an engaging storyline and rich language. We use *Those Darn Squirrels*, by Adam Rubin.

✔ Keep chart paper or a white board nearby for jotting children's ideas about their reading.

✔ Establish partnerships, if you have not done so already.

Session 2

✔ Write questions to guide discussion on a white board or chart paper.

✔ Display the anchor chart from Bend III, "Authors Have Intentions—So Pay Attention!" ✋

✔ Start an accountable talk chart to provide students with language stems to support their ability to share ideas and questions when discussing the text. You'll want to build on the chart students may have used in first grade.

✔ Keep chart paper or a white board nearby for jotting children's ideas about their reading.

Getting Ready: BOOK SELECTION

You will want to read many books with your class this month, sometimes through shared reading and other times through read-aloud. During shared reading, you will share books with your children that are just a bit above the level of the books they are reading on their own. Shared-reading texts will give you the opportunity to explore many of the reading challenges that are just ahead for readers. In read-aloud, on the other hand, you will want to stretch your students' thinking skills. Therefore, your read-aloud title will likely be at a level closer to end-of-the-year standards and sometimes a bit beyond (M/N/O). By working with a complex text in a read-aloud, children will be challenged to do more thinking to make sense of the story. This thinking work will expose young readers to more complex vocabulary and characters who have not only external problems (*I lost my dog*) but internal struggles (*I'm lonely*), as well.

Careful text selection will be key. You'll want to select texts that will grab your students' attention, push them to think about issues and ideas, and give them something to talk about in the classroom and on the playground. These books will likely be ones that contain rich language and generate interesting conversation. The whole-class reading, talking, and listening work that will go along with your read-aloud teaching will pave the way for

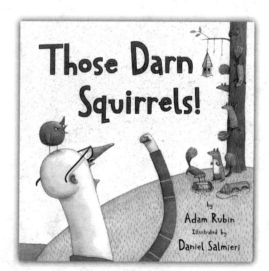

Those Darn Squirrels, by Adam Rubin, illustrated by Daniel Salmieri

the complexity of thought and the facility with comprehension skills that readers will need in the future. Additionally, you'll find that reading aloud is one of the quickest and most effective ways to build a literate community in your classroom.

In addition to a rich storybook like the one we have chosen for this unit, *Those Darn Squirrels*, we recommend that at least some of the books you read aloud during this unit are fairy tales (*The Three Little Pigs*, by Paul Galdone, and *Jack and the Beanstalk*, by Steven Kellogg, perhaps) as well as some fractured tales (*The Three Little Wolves and the Big Bad Pig*, by Eugene Trivizas, and *The True Story of the Three Little Pigs*, by Jon Scieszka).

You'll also want to read aloud chapter books early in the year. Because most of your students will be reading early chapter books, they will benefit from your model. Be sure that as you pick up these titles day after day, you showcase how to ready yourself to read further into the book. For example, you might demonstrate how you reread your Post-it notes and think back over the big events in the book, and then preview the next chapter before you begin the day's reading. We suggest that one of your first chapter book read-alouds could be *Mercy Watson to the Rescue*, by Kate DiCamillo (level K). Then, in shared reading, you could take one chapter from this text to study across a week, releasing more of the responsibility for reading the book to the children.

If you choose *Mercy Watson to the Rescue*, and it is only a level or so above most of your students' independent levels, we suggest you also choose a few chapter books with greater text complexity to read aloud. You might choose books like the Stink or Judy Moody series of books by Megan McDonald or the Ivy & Bean series by Annie Barrows. These texts are all level M/N and thus represent the kind of reading comprehension children will need to do independently by year's end.

In this early part of the year, you will want to focus your read-aloud work on helping children to develop comprehension muscles for determining important parts in a text, retelling, understanding characters, and beginning to build theories about those characters. Additionally, you will want children to work on their understanding of how an author conveys lessons to the reader.

We suggest you read this book aloud at least once during Bend I. Session 7, at the start of Bend II, relies on students being familiar with this text. We also suggest you revisit it often to support your students in practicing additional skills. The first read-aloud session described here is designed to come early in the unit, when you are first introducing the read-aloud. In the first session you will also support retelling and prediction skills. The second session is designed to come later in the unit, after you have already read the book with students at least one time. It is designed to support readers as they notice how the author makes each part of the text fit together. Further, children will work to think about the lessons the author works to convey. It is designed to be taught in Bend III, after you have introduced students to the chart "Authors Have Intentions—So Pay Attention!"

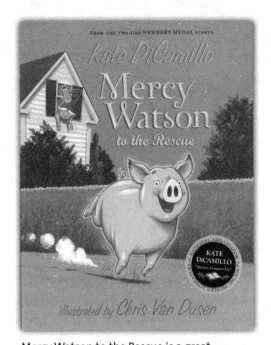

Mercy Watson to the Rescue is a great beginning-of-the-year read-aloud. After reading and discussing the whole text, we suggest you choose a chapter to work with in shared reading.

BEFORE YOU READ

Model how you take a sneak peek to preview. Then, invite children to think and react as they listen.

Call students to the rug and ask them to sit next to the partners they work with during reading workshop. With great fanfare, introduce your new read-aloud: "This book is called *Those Darn Squirrels*, and it is written by Adam Rubin and illustrated by Daniel Salmieri. Take a look at the cover, and I'm sure you can see that this is going to be a *funny* book! You see the man in the picture? He is yelling, 'Those darn squirrels!' and shaking his fist. Can you do it with me? Funny, right?!

"Let's study this cover a bit more. Who else do you see here? What do you think is happening? Turn and talk!" Move around the meeting area to listen in as partnerships talk.

Give children a minute to discuss what is happening on the cover, and then draw them back together to think about how the title *wants* to be read. Rehearse reading the title a few ways.

"So many of you noticed that there is a bird on the man's head, and it looks like the man and the bird are *both* yelling. Others of you said you thought the squirrels were eating all of the food out of the bird feeders in the tree. That must be why the man and the bird are yelling, right?

"How do you think the author wants us to sound when we read this title? Let's try it a few ways to see which sounds best!" Coach your students as they try out the title in different voices, perhaps an angry voice, a silly voice, and an annoyed voice.

Continue your sneak peek as you turn to the back cover and read the blurb. Retell what you learned in the blurb about the book while inviting children to join you and check your work.

Flip the book over and read aloud the blurb on the back cover. "Wow! This blurb really tells us a lot about what will happen in this story, right? I'm going to try to retell what I learned. I'll put up a finger for each important part, and will you do the same, checking to be sure I get all the important information?

"Here I go. Old Man Fookwire—what a funny name!—really likes painting pictures of birds. *But* he gets really sad when they fly south for the winter. *So*, he makes a plan to put out bird feeders to get the birds to stay. *The problem* is some hungry creatures—I bet those are the squirrels—want the birdseed too! Hmm, . . . I think that's all they tell us. Do you agree?

"Oh, yeah, the blurb also says the book is hilarious. That means 'extra funny'! I believe that! Look at these funny pictures and the funny name of the main character! Let's all say his name together!"

Rehearsing the character's name a few times will help children speak with ease about the character, and thus encourage the use of proper nouns rather than pronouns.

Invite the children to retell what they just learned from the blurb and the front cover and then to predict what will happen in the rest of the story.

"Readers, before we get started with this book, will you please retell what you know about how the story will begin and then predict with your partner what will happen next? Remember to retell across your fingers, like I did, and then add on with a prediction. Turn and talk!"

Listen in on your students' responses and use this time to assess both their retelling *and* their predictions. You might use the following as a checklist as you observe your students discussing the text.

Retelling

- Are students retelling sequentially?

- Are students using the character's name to retell?

- Are students naming the problem the character will face?

- Are students self-correcting when they realize they left out a part and therefore their retell does not make sense?

Predicting

- Are students predicting what will happen at the end?

- Are students predicting solutions that match the problem?

- Are students predicting only what will happen next?

- Are students predicting the middle and the end of the story?

- Do students include characters' feelings in their predictions?

AS YOU READ

Read aloud the text with expression, reacting to the text as you read. Encourage children to join you as you act out bits of the text to further engage students.

Begin your read-aloud looking closely at the title page. Though it looks like the cover, take a moment to think out loud about what you see in the illustration and to act out the bit of the story depicted here. You might say, "There is Old

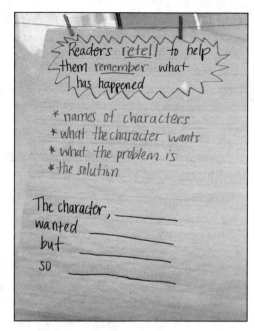

A chart can help children remember how to keep their retells short.

Man Fookwire with that bird on his head again. They each have an arm in the air and they seem to be threatening the squirrel. Oh, and it seems like the title is almost their speech bubble, saying, 'Those darn squirrels!'" You can act out the motion and invite the children to do so with you, saying the title together again with over-the-top expression.

As you flip through the next few pages, you might also think aloud about the pictures you see, commenting, "Oh, those must be Old Man Fookwire's paintings of the birds. There are a lot of them. I bet he paints all the time."

Pages 4–6: Read the next few pages, emphasizing details that bring out the point that the character is old and grumpy. React as you read and invite children to react with you. Then guide children as they check their sneak peek.

As you read, linger on the details that help you understand the main character. You might say, "Wow! Old Man Fookwire *is old*. I mean, dust comes out when he sneezes. Yuck! And who hates pies? What a grump!"

At the end of page 6 give children a moment to reflect on their sneak peek and then list what they have learned about the character so far. You might say, "Let's retell what we have learned about Old Man Fookwire so far. Put up a finger for each piece of information you have. See if you and your partner can name at least four things!"

Listen in to this turn-and-talk. Start to think about the children who are talking to each other and assess whether they are well matched as talk partners. If one seems to talk far more than the other, coach the talkative one to ask more questions, so that the quieter partner can find her voice.

"Well, it seems like our sneak peek was right on!"

Pages 7–10: Invite children to listen for more information about the character *and* to look out for information about new characters, and then continue reading. Pause briefly to chart what students are learning about characters.

You might say, "As we read the next few pages, listen for new information about our character, but don't stop there. Readers, new characters will be introduced soon and you'll want to collect information about them, too!" After a page or two, prompt kids to turn and talk. You might invite them to retell the story thus far.

SESSION 1: AS YOU READ

pp. 7–10: Invite children to listen for information about the characters. Pause briefly to ask what children are learning.

"As we read, listen for new information about the character, but don't stop there. New characters will be introduced soon, and you'll want to collect information about them, too!"

Then make a list of what they know about one character and then the others. You might generate a list like this:

Old Man Fookwire

- lives in an old house on the edge of town
- OLD
- grumpy (hates pies and puppies)
- so old he sneezes dust
- LOVES birds
- likes painting even though he isn't very good
- gets sad when the birds leave

The Squirrels

- like bird feeders and birdseed
- people think they're geniuses (make kites, good at math)

After this work, you might choose to have children predict again, or you could model higher-level prediction work that incorporates retelling and prediction. You could say, "Wow! So, we already know that Old Man Fookwire hates almost everything, but he *loves* those birds and he *loves* painting them. *But* the birds fly south each year, and that makes Old Man Fookwire quite sad. When he tries to feed them to get them to stay, the squirrels enter the story and eat lots of the food. Now the book says those squirrels are super smart, so I bet Fookwire and the squirrels are going to keep trying to outsmart each other! I wonder who will win."

Pages 11–12: Read to the end of the page and pause. Give children opportunities to act out this bit of text, elaborating on their ideas about the conflict.

Continue reading aloud to the end of page 12. Make sure that children are taking notice of the conflict here, because it is at the heart of the story. You might set up your students' thinking by saying, "Well, the old man sure does like those birds, and he is pretty mad that the squirrels might ruin his plans to keep them around through the winter. Partner 1, be Old Man Fookwire. Tell the squirrels why you are mad. Partner 2, will you be the squirrels? What do you think they want to say back? Go ahead!"

Listen in as students talk. Again, you'll want to help partners keep their conversations going without allowing one child to dominate. You might also coach children to refer to the text—to use words from the text in their conversations or to make their point by naming back what happened in a particular one part.

Fookwire	Squirrels
• lives in an old house on the edge of town • OLD • grumpy (hates pies and puppies) • so old he sneezes dust • LOVES birds • likes painting even though he isn't very good • gets sad when the birds leave	• like bird feeders and birdseed • people think they're geniuses (make kites, good at math)

Partner 1— Fookwire	Partner 2— Squirrels

Pages 13–19: Read on, stopping periodically to give children opportunities to act out bits of text and retell. With each retell, coach students to help each other in making the retell accurate but concise.

As you read, you might sprinkle the text with reactions that help children track the story. For example, you might say, "Oh my! It seems the problem is getting worse. Turn and retell to your partner what has happened up until now and what just happened to make things even *worse*."

Or you might say, "This part seems important. Act it out with your partner and then retell. Remember, a strong retell will give important information without naming every detail. Partners, help each other!" Listen in and coach students as they work.

Pages 19–23: Stop reading to give children a chance to clarify meaning with a partner. Then prompt children to talk about how the story will be resolved.

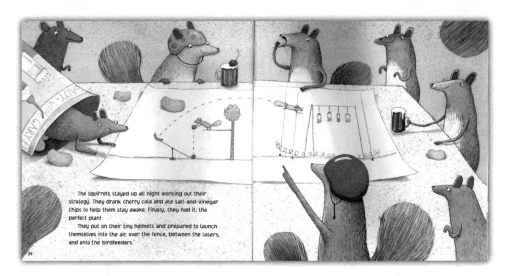

The squirrels stayed up all night working out their strategy. They drank cherry cola and ate salt-and-vinegar chips to help them stay awake. Finally, they had it: the perfect plan!

They put on their tiny helmets and prepared to launch themselves into the air, over the fence, between the lasers, and onto the birdfeeders.

At this pivotal point in the story, give children a moment to tell each other what just happened and to revise their predictions for the end of the book. You might say, "Oh my! I didn't think that would happen. Turn and tell your partner what just happened—and make sure you agree!" Listen in to be sure children understand the important events of this page, coaching children to notice when they disagree about the events of the book, thus moving them toward clarity.

Then voice over for children to revise their predictions for the end of the book. "Now that the birds have left for the winter, what do you think will happen next? Turn and talk!"

Pages 24–27: Continue reading, and then invite children to have a brief conversation with their partners about the characters.

Read a few more pages, and then pause your reading again. Give children a brief moment to discuss the change in the characters' actions. You might lead the children into their talk by saying, "Wow! The squirrels just did something unexpected, huh? How did they change? Is this what you thought would happen? How do you think Old Man Fookwire will react?"

Read to the end of the book, and give the children one last opportunity to act out the text, taking on the characters' thoughts.

"Readers, take a look at Old Man Fookwire now! It seems like the squirrels are not the only ones who changed! Partner 2, will you be Old Man Fookwire? And Partner 1, you act out the part of the squirrels. Characters, tell each other what you are thinking now!"

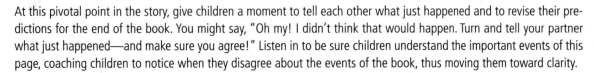

Partner 2— Fookwire	Partner 1— Squirrels

AFTER YOU READ

Move the children into a circle to facilitate whole-class conversation. Invite students to collaboratively retell the book as you turn the pages.

"What a funny story. So much happened, and some of it was really unexpected, too! Before we start talking about this book, will you quickly move into a circle so that we can all see each other as we talk about the book?"

Help your students move quickly into the new configuration, voicing over as children solve their own problems with finding space. A moment or two helping children to negotiate on their own now will save you lots of time later. You will want to situate yourself just outside of the circle, thus suggesting your role as a supporter of conversation, not the center of it.

"Now that you can all see each other, let's retell the book *together*. I'll flip through a few pages and then pause. If you want to retell that part, you can indicate that with a thumb on your knee. I will choose the first person to speak, but after that, you can call on the person who will speak after you."

Having the children call on each other will encourage them to listen and talk to each other rather than directing all their attention to you. As the year goes on, you will likely teach children to enter a conversation without calling on each other, but for now this is a step in that direction. You might go on to say, "Readers listen carefully to each other. You may want to clarify or add on to or even revise someone's retelling of a part."

Discuss how parts of the book *want* to be read.

"Readers, now that we all agree on how this story goes, I am thinking about the work you have been doing in reading workshop. You have been thinking so much about how your own books *want* to be read, and I am wondering if we might do that work with this book. too.

"Do you think this is a book that *wants* to be read in just one way, or might we read different parts in different ways?" Give children a moment to think before you continue. "Take a moment to talk to your partner: How do you think this book *wants* to be read, and which parts should we try out reading now?" Listen in to your students, and choose a part or two on which children want to focus their thinking work.

Reread a suggested portion of the text, talk about it how it *wants* to be read, and then read it together. Follow this work by having children act out the part.

Flip to the part of the text students suggested and where you know this work will pay off. You might say, "So many of you wanted to talk about this part. I'll read this part again, and as I do will you think about two questions: How does this part *want* to be read? How do you know?"

After you reread the part children have chosen to focus on, choose a child to start the conversation. Remind children that they will choose the person who talks next. Many teachers find it helpful to have three guidelines for this procedure: (1) Choose someone in less than three seconds. (2) Choose someone who indicated that she wants to speak. (3) Choose someone who has not yet spoken.

Your role in this work is to keep the conversation going. When the children seem to stop offering new ideas or thoughts, you can add in or ask a question, or you can move on to acting out the part. You might say, "It seems that you have sorted out how this text *wants* to be read. Let's read it that way together and then act it out." Place the text on the document camera and have children read with you, *or* if you think the text is simply too much of a stretch for the majority of your class, invite children to coach you as you read. You can close out the read-aloud by inviting a few kids to act out the part.

SESSION 2

BEFORE YOU READ

Before reading the book again, give children a chance to share all the reasons they like to reread books.

Gather your readers in the meeting area. "Readers, you all remember *Those Darn Squirrels*, right? I know you do because, ever since we read it the first time, I have heard you talking about it and saying the title in funny Old Man Fookwire voices and borrowing it from our classroom library anytime there is a free moment! So today I thought we would read it *again*!

"Right now, take a moment to tell your partner why you like to reread books—and maybe add why you are excited to reread *this* book!"

Even if your children have not been quite this enthusiastic about a book, letting them know that others are excited lifts the energy for rereading. You will also want to take this I-know-you-like-to-reread tact because it helps build enthusiasm where it might not grow on its own. As you listen in to the partnerships, keep the tone of excitement going. Encourage children to think about books they have read over and over and about the parts of those books and this book that they love.

Invite children to retell once more to offer additional support with retelling and to remind students of the overall story.

If you still have a significant number of children who are struggling to give strong and concise retells, you might spend a little extra time here coaching and coming up with a whole-class retell of the book. Otherwise, this retell will really just serve to remind the children of the story as a whole, since this read-aloud may come days—or even a week or two—after your first read of the story.

SESSION 2 : BEFORE YOU READ

Cover: Before reading the book again, have children share the reasons they like to reread books.

"Readers, you all remember this book, right? I know this one is a favorite of yours. Right now, take a moment to tell your partner why you like to reread books. Maybe add why you are excited to reread *this* book!"

Let children know that as you read today, they need to be thinking deeply about how the text fits together and what the lesson (or lessons) might be that the author is trying to teach.

"Readers, now that we have the whole story in our minds, let's dig a little deeper with this text. You have been working hard in your reading time to think about your authors and their intentions, right? Well, I thought we could do some more of that work together today." Then, you might choose to read your "Authors Have Intentions—So Pay Attention!" chart for reference.

"As we read this book today, let's think about two things authors do to make their writing masterful. I've written a few questions on the white board to help us do just that."

- How does the author make this story fit together? Which parts of this story fit together? WHY?

- What lesson is the author trying to teach? Which parts of the story show the lesson? Is there more than one lesson?

"As I read this book to you today, will you keep asking yourself these questions? And if you get to a part that you think is really important, let me know by giving me a thumbs up so I can give you a chance to chat with your partner about that part." Of course, you will not stop your reading every time a child has an idea, but you will find that when a bunch of children have thoughts, it is best to give them a chance to share. This will help them hold on to those ideas, and it will give you an opportunity to understand the parts of texts they are cueing in on.

AS YOU READ

Read the story with expression, incorporating any work you did last time on how the books *wants* to be read. Emphasize parts of the book you initially read past.

Begin rereading the book to students, reading with expression. Pay particular attention to parts you studied during your earlier whole-class conversation, pointing out that you remember how the book wants you to read those parts. Then, model reading them based on how they want to be read.

Be sure also to sprinkle in thoughts about things you didn't notice on the first read. You might say, "Oh! I didn't catch that the first time. He lives far from other people. Now I'm thinking about how that goes with everything that comes later, how he is a grump and doesn't like anyone but the birds!" You can also read a page and then say, "Wait! I didn't really notice the first time that it says they ate only *some* of the bird food. I think I want to read this part a little differently now."

Page 12: Pause reading here to give children a chance to think about how the story fits together so far.

"Readers, we have read a good bit of this story already, and I bet you're noticing some parts that fit together. Turn and discuss these questions with your partner: How does the author make this story fit together? Which parts of this story fit together? Why?" Kneel down and coach students to lift the level of their work.

As children talk, get a feel for how well they are putting parts of the text together. Use the questions and sample student responses below as a guide while you listen. Jot down notes you can use to inform later conferences, small groups, and read-alouds.

- Are they noticing that information about the characters unfolds across this part of the book?

    Example, "Wow! I didn't realize the first time that the squirrels kind of get worse. At first they take only some, but then when Old Man Fookwire is mean, they take more!"

- Are they thinking about parts that come later and noticing how these early pages fit?

    Example, "The squirrels might be geniuses now, but their plan doesn't work later."

- Are they thinking about characters they didn't consider on the first read?

    Example, "The birds just take the food. They are never really *nice* to Fookwire."

- Are they able to name specific parts of the text to compare?

    Example, "The squirrels are geniuses on all the parts. Like they are geniuses when they say they can make a box kite and they are geniuses when they figure out how to get the food from the first feeder *and* the second feeder!"

Pages 16–17: Invite partnerships to consider the lesson (or lessons) that the author is teaching.

"Readers, you know that authors really like to teach the reader a lesson—or two! Take a minute to think about these questions: What lesson is the author trying to teach? Which parts of the story show the lesson? Is there more than one lesson?"

Give the children a moment to think alone before directing them to talk to a partner.

"Retell the story so far with your partner so it's fresh in your head, and then discuss these questions for a moment. Don't forget to tell which parts of the text go with your ideas!" As you listen in, again you will want to take note of what children are saying as you coach them:

- Are children thinking of lessons that match the text?

- Are children referring to the text as they name the lessons?

- Are children thinking about a lesson that goes with just one page? Or does the lesson relate to just one part? Or does it relate to the book as a whole?

- Are the children naming lessons the character is learning? Or can they name lessons the *reader* is learning?

Read to the end of the story, stopping a few more times for children to think about how the story fits together and what lessons they are finding in the text.

Stop every few pages to give quick prompts for children to consider the story and the lessons it conveys. You may find that it is helpful to name out a few of the lessons children are sharing with each other and then invite other children to think about whether they see that lesson emerging as well. This will prime their thinking for the end conversation. Be sure not to do any whole-class discussion now, however, because you will want to build energy for a longer conversation at the end of the book.

AFTER YOU READ

Invite the children to begin a whole-class conversation about the read-aloud book.

Once the children are in a circle, reread the questions you jotted on the white board or chart paper at the start of the read-aloud. Invite one child to offer some ideas to get the conversation started.

Your role in class conversation will evolve quickly. In the time since you read this book the first time, your children have likely learned how to move from one speaker to the next with relative ease. Now that you do not need to facilitate the management of the conversation, you will want to support your readers in deepening their discussions of text. You might find that tapping the talk chart reminds children of ways to add to the conversation that go beyond repeating what another child has said. Or you may find that whispering words of encouragement to children who have ideas but don't readily offer them will deepen the conversations.

Start a chart to list the lessons children are discussing. Coach in to lift the level of conversation and help students strengthen the lessons they suggest.

As children share ideas and thoughts about the book, you might start a quick chart to hold the lessons children are naming and discussing in the text. You might say, "It sounds like Joey is suggesting a lesson from the text. I'm going to jot it right here so that we can all see it. Joey, let me know if I have it right."

Then you can note how long children are discussing one idea before moving to the next. When children shift to a new lesson, voice that over too. You might say, "It sounds like Leila is suggesting a different lesson in this text, right? I am going to jot it here." Children will likely move quickly from one lesson to the next for a while, and this is okay. Think of it as a way to get a lot of ideas on the table before you focus the children toward one line of thinking.

Make sure that as you jot ideas on the board, you support the children in reflecting on whether the lessons they name are ones for the reader or just for the character. The class can work together to reword lessons that apply only to the characters. For example, one child might offer the lesson "If you can't paint birds, you can paint squirrels." You might engage the class in revising this idea by asking, "Can we say that another way so that it is not just a lesson for Fookwire but a lesson for us, too?" Then aid the children in changing it to something more like this: "If you can't get what you want, try something different."

Focus the conversation. Support children to stay with one idea and discuss its merits across the text.

Once there are a few lessons on your board, invite your children to choose one to talk about for a while. You can say, "Let's look over the list of lessons we have here. Which one should we think about some more? We want to find one that feels like it can fit the *whole* story. Then we can discuss all the parts in the book that work to teach that one lesson." Let the children turn and talk, coaching them toward a choice that you think will yield a strong discussion and lots of opportunity to go back to the book.

Then reread the lesson you will discuss together and choose someone to start this part of the conversation. As the conversation gets underway, make sure that children are adding to each other's ideas, referring to the text, and asking for clarification when they seem confused. If the conversation gets quiet quickly, you can say, "Readers, let's pause for a moment. Think. If you were the next person to talk, what would you say?" After giving the children a moment to think quietly, invite them to share with their partners. This is a great way of giving children a reflective moment and a practice space for their talk. Then invite someone to restart the conversation. Often this is all that is needed to buoy their energy and get ideas flowing again.

Support students in revising the lesson they are discussing so it fits better with the book.

When you are ready to bring the conversation to a close, invite children to say whether they think the lesson under discussion did, in fact, hold up across the text. Then give the class an opportunity to rewrite the lesson to make it an even better fit. You might say, "Now that you have discussed the idea 'Don't be mean right away. Give new people a chance,' do you think there is another way to say it that would fit better with everything you have found in the book?'"

Don't spend too much time debating each word. Instead, offer a few rewrites and then choose quickly. "It sounds like you mostly agree that we can say this best with 'Don't be quick to judge new people. New friends can be anywhere.' Great! Let's put that on a Post-it on the cover of the book!"

SESSION 2: AFTER YOU READ

End (p. 32): Support children to focus on one idea and discuss its merits across the text.

"Let's look over the list of lessons we have here. Which one should we think about some more? We want to find one that feels like it can fit the *whole* story. Then we can discuss all the parts in the book that work to teach that one lesson."

Shared Reading

Readers Grow Stronger

Text Selections

› *Mercy Watson to the Rescue*, by Kate DiCamillo, illustrated by Chris Van Dusen

› Song of your choice, for example "There Was an Old Lady Who Swallowed a Fly"

The beginning of the school year is prime time for creating a community of readers. In second grade, one of the best ways to build community is with comedy. So when you set out to choose texts for shared reading, you will do well to find humorous ones. Since shared reading is a time to work with children on stretching their ability to word solve, comprehend, and read with fluency all at once, you'll also want to choose a text that is just beyond your students' ability to read independently. For most second-graders at the beginning of the year, this means that you will seek out books at level K or L. Since songs are rarely leveled, you will want to choose a text that poses some challenges, both in the words and for meaning making. We recommend a familiar song like "There Was an Old Lady Who Swallowed a Fly" because it is both fun and will stretch your students to read a longer text with some tricky language. You may choose to write this song on chart paper, though you could also use one of many illustrated book versions of the song and display it on your document camera. Either way, this song will act as the warm-up for the more in-depth work you will do with the focus text.

We chose *Mercy Watson to the Rescue* as the focus text because it is an early chapter book, and most of your students will read chapter books in a month or so. (We also chose it because it's FUNNY!) This text is commonly leveled at K, though some believe that because of the humor and complexity of the jokes it could even fit the criteria for a level L text. This makes it a perfect match for most second-grade classrooms at this time of year. You will want to read the whole of *Mercy Watson to the Rescue* as a read-aloud *before* you use it as a shared reading text. Shared reading will likely take about fifteen minutes a day, and each day you will want to reread the same section of the text, studying it in a different way. Therefore, you will want to choose one chapter to read across the week. We have chosen to focus on Chapter 3 because it contains the central problem (or confusion) that drives the rest of the story and provides lots of opportunities for word solving and fluency work.

DAY ONE: Warm Up, Book Introduction, and First Read

To start your shared reading for the week, we suggest you introduce a song and a book. Both of these texts will be used in shared reading throughout the week, so that children gain familiarity with them. The song will act as a warm-up text, helping the children to work on fluency skills, such as pacing, parsing text, and using prosodic cues to read with appropriate expression. With the song, you will want to emphasize how the class can sing with one strong, clear voice that punctuates the meaning of the text. You will want to guide children to read as you point to the beginning of each line of the text. This pointing will help children track the text down the page, thus teaching them how to track print in their own books. Pointing under each word is counter to your purpose at this level, because it will instead make the children's eyes move one word at a time across the line.

Then, introduce students to a book. Since this will be the children's first time looking at the words in the text, it is the right time to practice the orchestration of all three sources of information—meaning, syntax, and visual information (MSV)—to work through difficult words. As you get ready for the lesson, choose a few words to cover with Post-its or highlighter tape. Choose words that match the kind of words your students grapple with on their own or that reinforce the work being done in reading workshop. So, if you are seeing many children struggling to work with complex vowel teams, cover words where utilizing vowel teams will be the key to decoding. Be sure that you also encourage a strong reading process, in which children think about the meaning of a word *before* they decode, and then check their guess to make sure it makes sense, sounds right, and looks right. Finally, be sure that the class rereads any sentence where they engaged in word solving to be sure it works.

When you come to the end of the read, you will want to turn your focus to comprehension work that connects to your unit of study in reading workshop. For example, you might choose to do some retelling work.

DAY ONE FOCUS

✔ Build a community of readers who work together to read and think about beloved texts.

✔ Engage students in some word solving as they draw on strategies they used last year (and are learning this fall) while orchestrating the use of meaning, syntax, and visual information (MSV).

GETTING READY

✔ Prepare a copy of a silly song to sing with students. We recommend "There Was an Old Lady Who Swallowed a Fly." Make sure the copy is large enough for students all to read, or be ready to project it (see Warm Up).

✔ Prepare to share a chapter from a familiar text a level or two above the reading level of most of your students. We suggest Chapter 3 from *Mercy Watson to the Rescue*, by Kate DiCamillo (see Book Introduction and First Reading).

✔ Display the text, possibly on a document camera (see Warm Up and Book Introduction and First Read).

✔ Cover four to five words in the chapter you select. We recommend primarily covering nouns and verbs. Be sure the first few words are fully covered, but partially cover the last two words so that only the first few letters are showing (see Book Introduction and First Read).

WARM UP: *"There Was an Old Lady Who Swallowed a Fly"*

Sing a familiar song (or read a chant, poem, or chart) a few times to build confidence, excitement, and fluency.

Project a copy of "There Was an Old Lady Who Swallowed a Fly" or display the text on chart paper. Invite children to sing with you as you sing a silly song, pointing to the beginning of each line of text as you sing. You might say, "I bet many of you have heard this song before. Let's work together to sing it loud and proud, even when it is a bit silly. Ready?!"

> *There was an old lady who swallowed a fly*
> *I don't know why she swallowed a fly—Perhaps she'll die!*
>
> *There was an old lady who swallowed a spider,*
> *That wriggled and wiggled and tiggled inside her;*
> *She swallowed the spider to catch the fly;*
> *I don't know why she swallowed a fly—Perhaps she'll die!*

There was an old lady who swallowed a bird;
How absurd to swallow a bird.
She swallowed the bird to catch the spider,
She swallowed the spider to catch the fly;
I don't know why she swallowed a fly—Perhaps she'll die!

There was an old lady who swallowed a cat;
Fancy that to swallow a cat!
She swallowed the cat to catch the bird,
She swallowed the bird to catch the spider,
She swallowed the spider to catch the fly;
I don't know why she swallowed a fly—Perhaps she'll die!

There was an old lady who swallowed a dog;
What a hog, to swallow a dog;
She swallowed the dog to catch the cat,
She swallowed the cat to catch the bird,
She swallowed the bird to catch the spider,
She swallowed the spider to catch the fly;
I don't know why she swallowed a fly—Perhaps she'll die!

There was an old lady who swallowed a cow,
I don't know how she swallowed a cow;
She swallowed the cow to catch the dog,
She swallowed the dog to catch the cat,
She swallowed the cat to catch the bird,
She swallowed the bird to catch the spider,
She swallowed the spider to catch the fly;
I don't know why she swallowed a fly—Perhaps she'll die!

There was an old lady who swallowed a horse . . .
She's dead, of course!

Sing the song twice, perhaps even three times, to make sure that everyone is participating. You might need to offer a few words of encouragement to get everyone involved, but a little extra effort now will pay off throughout the year. Getting kids engaged early will help children feel comfortable reading together, even when they trip over their words and make mistakes. Laugh this off, give a little added support, and then give the children a chance to try again.

You can make a game of reading the long-winded parts a few times until everyone can sing them it well. You might say, "Phew!! It is hard to read that *whole* part and still keep the tune going! Let's try it again. Take a *big* breath, now let go!" To the children, this will be lots of fun, but you'll know that really you are helping them to scoop up more words in one breath and thus improving their fluency.

BOOK INTRODUCTION AND FIRST READING
Mercy Watson to the Rescue, Chapter 3, by Kate DiCamillo

Give a book introduction that situates readers to the portion of the book you will read and builds excitement for the work ahead.

Create excitement for today's shared reading. This book will be one that you can use across the year in shared reading as well as in reading workshop during your series unit and in writing workshop as a mentor text. You will want children not only to enjoy the book but also know it well enough to use throughout the year for these various purposes.

As you place the book on the document camera, you might say, "Readers, I know how much you all *loved* reading *Mercy Watson to the Rescue* during our read-aloud time, so I thought we could read it together in shared reading, too!" Your enthusiasm for this work will be contagious, so be a little dramatic. Lead the kids in a cheer or clap your hands excitedly and invite the children to join you.

You might go on to add, "Since we read the whole book together already, I picked just the most exciting chapter for us to work on—Chapter 3!"

Open the book to the first page of Chapter 3, revealing the picture in which Mr. and Mrs. Watson's bed is beginning to fall through an ever-widening hole in the floor. You can point to the first word in the chapter, which reads, "BOOM!" Then you might say, "This is a super exciting chapter because this is when the action *really* begins in this book. This chapter is also when a lot of the confusion starts, so I thought it would be a great part for us to reread."

Model retelling the first part of the book, and invite students to retell as well.

"Before we do, though, let's get ourselves oriented in the book. This is Chapter 3, so we will need to start with a retell that helps us remember what the story is about and what happened in Chapters 1 and 2. Ready?" You can choose to have the children retell the earlier chapters with their reading partners while you listen in, using the information you collect as informal assessment, or you can choose to model the retell.

If you choose to model the retell you might say, "I'm sure you remember how this story goes, so will you listen and check to see if you agree with my retell of the first part of this story? Great! Here I go." Model retelling across your fingers. "This is a story about a pig named Mercy Watson. Mercy lives with Mr. and Mrs. Watson and, even though she is a pig, they treat her like she is their daughter. In the first chapter, Mr. and Mrs. Watson are putting Mercy to bed and they are singing her a lullaby. But when they leave Mercy in the dark of her own room she gets scared and can't sleep. In the second chapter, Mercy jumps into bed with the Watsons. They are all dreaming. Mr Watson is dreaming of driving a race car. Mercy is dreaming of eating enormous piles of toast with a great deal of butter on it, and Mrs. Watson is dreaming of making all that toast for Mercy." You can flip through the pages of the first few chapters as you do this, or simply have children think with you as you model. Either way, give the students a chance to retell it themselves, after your model.

Invite children to consider how the chapter *wants* to be read.

Before you jump into reading, engage children in thinking about how the text *wants* to be read. You might say, "Second-graders, we don't need to do most of our sneak peek work, because we have read this book before, *but* we can consider how this book *wants* to be read. We already know what kind of mood, or feeling, has been set up in this book, so let's think about what kind of voice we will use to read this chapter. Turn and talk!"

Your children will likely have no trouble confirming that the chapter requires a scary or suspenseful voice, even if those words do not come to them easily. You can coach them to come up with this language.

Read the chapter fluently, encouraging children to read along.

Read the chapter with expression and fluency, encouraging the children to read along right away. Be sure not to slow down your reading to read *with* your students. The purpose here is for readers to read with expression at a quick—but not rushed—clip. If you notice that your readers' voices are getting muffled through one portion, challenge them to reread it with you at your pace. You'll notice that they will gain confidence as they learn to keep up with you; perhaps even smiles and giggles will spread through the room!

Parsing text will also be a fluency challenge in this text. Most books at this level and at the levels below parse out the text, so that each line is a meaningful phrase. This book, however, wraps the text from one line to the next mid-phrase, thus requiring the reader to move from line to line, using punctuation and meaning to break up sentences and know when to take mid-sentence breaths. You may be tempted to point under each word to keep the readers together, but this will only stagnate their progress. Instead, point at the beginning of each line, or if you want children to pay closer attention to punctuation you can tap the punctuation as you read through each sentence.

When you reach one of the four or five covered words, pause and invite the class to practice cross-checking sources of information (MSV) when word solving.

As you read through the text for the first time, you will want to draw students' attention to a few covered words. Covering these words will ensure that the whole class can work together to word solve. The first few words should be nouns or verbs that occur in the later part of a sentence. For example, you might choose to cover the word *frightened* on page 14. As students read the sentence, they will need to anticipate and determine a word that would fit based on syntax, as well as meaning.

Your purpose here is not for children to "get it right" on the first try, but instead to try a few words and then figure out which works best. You may be tempted to reveal the word the first time a child yells it out; resist the urge. Narrate trying out each word, checking to make sure it makes sense and sounds right. Then you might say, "If the word is _____, what letters would you expect to see at the beginning? At the end? What vowels do you expect to see in the middle?" Go through this same process with a few other guesses before revealing the word and asking, "Which of your guesses matches the letter we see here?"

Once you have determined how to read the word, invite your class to reread the sentence with phrasing and fluency, putting the whole sentence back together within the text as a whole.

Later in the chapter, you might choose to cover only part of a word, thus encouraging children to decode the word part by part. For example, you might choose to work with the word *department* the first time it occurs on page 16, leaving the letters *de* at the beginning of the word uncovered. You will still encourage children to think about meaning and syntax, anticipating the word as they read, but now you will also support the use of visual information from the start. Make sure to read the sentence together, reading up to and including the part of the word that is revealed before having children guess. Then remind them to check. "Does that make sense? Does it sound right *and* look right?" Remember to always reread the sentence after the class has word solved, thus putting the sentence and the meaning of the text back together before reading on.

AFTER READING

End Day One with some brief comprehension work.

After reading this chapter with your students, you will want to comment on the excitement and suspense that it holds. You might say, "Wow! This chapter sure has a lot of action and feeling in it! With the person next to you, name what happened in your favorite part and how the characters were feeling!" This will get your students talking and recalling bits of the chapter right away.

Since you will return to this text across the week, you'll want to make sure that the children have a strong literal understanding of the events of the chapter *in sequence*. Therefore, you will likely close this first day by having children retell the chapter in order. You could choose to do this with the whole class, perhaps even doing some shared writing as your readers retell the chapter across five fingers. Alternatively, you could choose to have children retell to a partner as you move around the room coaching the retells and making notes for future small groups.

Either way, end your reading by getting the excitement up for your next read of the text. You might say, "What an exciting chapter! I can't wait to read it again tomorrow, when we will read it even better and study some of the trickiest words in the chapter!"

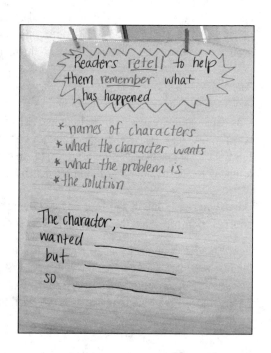

Readers retell to help them remember what has happened

* names of characters
* what the character wants
* what the problem is
* the solution

The character, _____
wanted _____
but _____
so _____

On Day Two, you'll reread both the song and the chapter from *Mercy Watson to the Rescue*. Use this read to focus on cross-checking words using all three sources of information. It is important that you prompt cross-checking behaviors both when children have miscued and occasionally when there is not a miscue. This is particularly crucial if you have many transitional readers, readers moving from level J through level M. You have likely found that these readers often make mistakes as they focus on reading quickly and frequently failing to notice and self-correct the mistakes they have made. Cross-checking during shared reading will slow down these readers and provide a vision of what monitoring sounds and looks like. You might say, "Wait, I'm not sure about that word. Let's check it."

Then you can lead children through the process of checking for all three sources of information. Many children in second grade are still unsure of the difference between checking with the three commonly used questions: Does it make sense? Does it sound right? Does it look right? You might find that it is helpful to add brief prompts for the questions. For example, you might say, "Does it make sense? What is happening in the book and in the picture? Does it sound right? What kind of word would fit here, a word that names a person or an action or another kind of word? Does it look right? Are those the letters that you expect to see?"

You will also want to make sure that children are using the appropriate decoding strategies for the levels they are reading. If your class is reading mostly on benchmark (level I/J/K), you'll want to coach them into reading words part by part, using increasingly complex spelling patterns to do so. They will also need to practice being flexible with vowel patterns (for example, *ea*, *ou*, *ow*), trying out a few sounds before finding the one that works.

Of course, as you work with children to monitor and word solve, you will also want their reading to gain fluency. Don't forget that after every time children check a word, you'll want them to reread to put the solved word into context.

WARM UP: *"There Was an Old Lady Who Swallowed a Fly"*

Sing a familiar song (or read a chant, poem, or chart) to build fluency.

Gather children in the meeting area to sing "There Was an Old Lady Who Swallowed a Fly." As you sing, note places where children hold a note to stress the importance or the absurdity of a word or phrase, and then prompt them to find other places where this will add to the meaning. Play with this a bit, having fun and pointing out how the tone of the song changes as you stress different parts.

You might also choose to sing one stanza as though the song is the sad story of a woman with an eating problem and another stanza as a ridiculous song about a silly woman. Playing with the way you sing this will help children to work on fluency while getting them ready for the more challenging work of determining how a book wants to be read.

DAY TWO FOCUS

✔ Reading for comprehension

✔ Pausing at tricky words to ask, "Does it make sense, sound right, and look right?" (cross-checking)

✔ Rereading to understand the larger story

GETTING READY

✔ Display a copy of the song you used yesterday. Here we sing "There Was an Old Lady Who Swallowed a Fly" (see Warm Up).

✔ Prepare to share a chapter from the familiar text you read yesterday with students. Here we reread Chapter 3 from *Mercy Watson to the Rescue* (see Second Reading).

✔ Use highlighter tape to cover a few words in your selected text that students will be able to solve by using meaning, syntax, and visual cues (see Second Reading).

✔ Create a chart titled "We Can Retell Well by . . ." and add three bullets to the chart: "Retelling across fingers," "Including characters, setting, and plot," and "Using words like *at the beginning*, *then*, *next*, *suddenly*, and *finally*" (see After Reading).

SECOND READING: *Mercy Watson to the Rescue*, Chapter 3, by Kate DiCamillo

Remind students of the work they did yesterday, and encourage them to cross-check tricky words to ensure they are reading with accuracy.

Before you read Chapter 3 again, remind children of the work they did yesterday to read the book with accuracy. You might say, "Readers, this chapter is packed with suspense and even a few laughs. When stories are exciting and fun, sometimes readers make mistakes without even noticing. Yesterday you worked hard to figure out the tricky words. Today, those tricky words will be a bit easier, but that doesn't mean reading will be purely smooth sailing. Get yourselves ready to *read*, to *enjoy*, *and* to *check*. You'll want to make sure your reading is correct!"

Invite students to reread the text with you. Highlight a few words to provide practice in cross-checking, and prompt students to use all three sources of information as they cross-check.

Begin reading the chapter with expression and fluency. Encourage all students to read along with you as you point to the beginning of each line.

While yesterday, you covered words you wanted children to work on, today you might choose to simply highlight a few words with highlighter tape. The highlighter tape will alert the children that this is a word to pay closer attention to, using meaning, syntax, *and* visual information simultaneously. You might say to children, "Today, I have highlighted a few words that you can check to make sure your reading is right. When we get to each of these words, I will stop reading, but you go ahead and read it. Then take a moment to check and prove to your partner that the word makes sense, sounds right, and looks right!"

This work can be trickier than it sounds. When you have children talk about each word, you may need to prompt them to be more specific. For example, you might prompt children to prove that the highlighted word *nonsense*, on page 14, "looks right." Many children will likely reply, "I know it says *nonsense* because it starts with an *n*!" Push the children to use more complex features. You'll want them to use word parts or vowel patterns or words within words as proof. When figuring out the word *wondered* on page 17, you might ask "Does it sound right?" Then you'll listen for children to say, "It sounds right because that is what Mercy is doing. She's wondering about the toast!" Or when children focus on the word *cannot* on page 16, you'll listen for children to say, "It makes sense because they want to call the fire department, but they cannot move. If they *could* move, there would be no problem!" Other children might notice the two smaller words, *can* and *not*. Of course you will ask all three questions each time children cross-check a word.

As you read on, you will want to repeat this process to give children a few opportunities to practice. You will also want to turn more of the reading responsibility over to your students. Let your voice trail off when possible and listen for your students' voices to get stronger. If the children stumble when you do this, use it as an opportunity for more cross-checking.

As you read, stopping to cross-check, don't forget about pace. This whole lesson should take about fifteen minutes. If you find that cross-checking the first few words is taking longer than you expect, remove the highlighter tape from some of the words. Keeping the pace brisk will ensure that your students stay engaged and thus learn more.

AFTER READING

Retell and make a connection to independent reading.

As you close up this lesson, you can choose to do a few different things. First and foremost, you'll want to have children retell. If their retelling yesterday was not as strong as you hoped, you might introduce a chart to support retelling. You can say, "Yesterday we worked hard to retell this chapter well. I listened in to your retelling and found that there were a few things you did to make your retellings clear. Take a look."

We Can Retell Well by . . .

- Retelling across fingers
- Including characters, setting, and plot
- Using words like <u>at the beginning</u>, <u>then</u>, <u>next</u>, <u>suddenly</u>, and <u>finally</u>

Then invite partners to retell again, using the chart to coach each other.

Draw a connection between the shared reading work students did and their independent reading work.

Before leaving the meeting area, be sure to make a connection between the work you have just done and the work children do when they read independently. You might say, "Readers, today you practiced two very important skills that strong readers practice as they grow: One, you checked your reading. Whenever you got to a tricky word, you checked to be sure that it made sense, sounded right, and looked right. Two, you did a quick retell after you read. These are both skills you'll want to practice when you read alone, too!"

DAY THREE: Word Study

On your third read of Chapter 3 from *Mercy Watson to the Rescue*, you can focus on bringing your word study work into shared reading. When readers are learning foundational skills in word study, it is important that they learn to integrate that knowledge into their reading of whole texts. Shared reading is a great opportunity for just that sort of integration.

You will likely want to highlight a small range of skills that you are teaching during word study time. You can plan for skills that stretch across the foundational skills, such as phonics, vocabulary, and fluency with high-frequency words. You'll want to use the information that you are gathering from your assessments to inform your focus here. Take a look at your spelling inventories, as well as your running records and word identification assessments to help you decide. Typically, transitional readers face greater challenges with inflectional endings, long vowel patterns, possessives, contractions, compound words, prefixes and suffixes, and more complex vocabulary. You may decide to focus heavily on one of these concepts or support a few across the text.

WARM UP: *"There Was an Old Lady Who Swallowed a Fly"*

Reread the song, quickly noticing some of the expressions and then asking students to generate possible meanings.

As you sing "There Was an Old Lady Who Swallowed a Fly" with your students today, you might choose to pause at two or three of the phrases that comment on the old woman's actions. You can encourage your students to sing these parts with extra expression and then give them a chance to define the expressions, as well. Idioms and sayings become a more frequent challenge for readers in levels K, L, and M, so a focus on noticing and beginning to define these will pay off over and over as your students move up levels throughout this year.

You might say, "Readers, there are some funny sayings used in this song to describe what the songwriter thinks about what the old woman does. As we read today, let's stop at a few of these and try to explain what they mean." Then when you get to phrases like "how absurd" and "fancy that" and "what a hog," you can call your students to action. You might say, "Wait a second. This says 'fancy that,' but I don't see anything *fancy* going on here! What do you think this expression means? Turn and talk!" There will be a great deal of work across the second-grade year—in both reading and writing—that requires children to think about, define, and use more complex expressions. Shared reading is a great forum for getting that work started.

THIRD READING: *Mercy Watson to the Rescue*, Chapter 3, by Kate DiCamillo

Reread the text with students for a third time, drawing students' attention to the word study focus you selected.

Invite students to reread the chapter with you with expression and fluency. As you point to the beginning of each line, look for opportunities to transfer more reading responsibility to students, and let your voice trail off as students' voices get stronger.

As you read with students, draw their attention to a word study focus you select using data from assessments. One foundational skill you might integrate is using spelling patterns to decode. You can cover *woke* and *hole* to emphasize the long vowel pattern *o-e*. Or you may wish to cover words with inflectional endings, such as *opened*, *hopped*, and *arguing*. You can also invite students to go on a word hunt for more words that end with the letters *ed* and *ing*.

Build vocabulary and start a Juicy Word Wall to encourage children to use the words in their conversations and writing, too!

Shared reading provides opportunities to teach kids strategies to understand unknown words and build vocabulary, as well. One way to highlight these words is to post a "juicy word" collection in your classroom, a wall of words that are interesting, fun to say, or useful to know for both reading and writing. Encourage children to add words to this collection as they come across words they want to remember.

GETTING READY

✔ Display a copy of the song you used yesterday. Here we sing "There Was an Old Lady Who Swallowed a Fly" (see Warm Up).

✔ Prepare to share a chapter from the familiar text you read yesterday with students. Here we reread Chapter 3 from *Mercy Watson to the Rescue* (see Third Reading).

✔ Choose a word study focus (or focuses) for today's rereading, based on the needs of your readers (see Third Reading).

✔ Start a Juicy Word Wall to support vocabulary development (see Third Reading).

✔ Highlight compound words that appear across the text (see Third Reading).

✔ Hang an empty pocket chart nearby, and be ready to add several root words from the text written on sentence strips. We suggest *escape*, *rescue*, and *gallop*. Also, be ready to add inflectional endings written on sentence strips, including *ing*, *ed*, and *s* (see After Reading).

For example, you might stop at the word *recalled* on page 17 and say, "That's an interesting word. Let's take a close look at it. I see a word in the middle, *call*. *Call* means 'to talk to someone or to find something.' My mom says, 'Let me *call* up that memory.' Let's look at other parts of the word, *re* at the beginning. Put that together with *call* and say that word—*recall*. What do you think that means?"

Don't stop there! Continue by pointing out the ending. You can say, "Don't forget the ending, *ed*. *Recalled*. As I run my finger under the word, let's read it together—*recalled*. How does the *ed* change the meaning of this word?" After children have discussed the meaning of each part and read the whole word, you might say, "Now turn to your partner, explain what *recalled* means, and describe something you have recalled." After giving partners a minute to talk, you might say, "Now let's add this word to our Juicy Word Wall collection, and be sure to use *recalled* when you are talking and writing."

Highlight compound words, and encourage students to use the smaller words making up the compound word to decode the bigger word.

Give children a chance to notice compound words in the text. You might highlight the word *earthquake* on page 14. You can say, "Readers, let's take a closer look at this word. This word is a compound word, which means it is one word that is made up of two smaller words. Those two smaller words help us to figure out how to pronounce *and* understand the meaning of the bigger word. Let's try this now!" Start by reading the word using the two smaller words to help children decode. Next, you can have the children talk about the meaning of the two smaller words and then what they mean together.

Starting with a word like *earthquake* is helpful because most of the children will already know its meaning but will now understand how to replicate this work with another word. You can continue to find compound words, such as *however*, *whatever*, *cannot*, and *bedroom*, throughout the chapter.

AFTER READING

Emphasize different root words from the text, and describe how adding an inflectional ending changes how you read a word and what the word means.

This is a good time for children to think about how word endings change the meaning of words. You can start this study by choosing some root words from the texts such as *escape*, *rescue*, and *gallop*, writing them on a sentence strip, and placing them in a pocket chart. Then add inflectional endings, such as *ing*, *ed*, and *s*. Discuss how an ending is an important part not only of reading a word but also of understanding what it means.

Give children a chance to explain these endings and the effects they have on words they are attached to. Children might say, "*Escaped* means that someone got away and now it is over, but *escapes* means that someone is getting away *right now*!" You might extend this work by giving partnerships a white board to share and then letting children play with root words by adding different endings.

The fourth day's focus in shared reading will revolve around fluency helping students to work on parsing, pacing, and using prosodic cues. This fluency work will also help students read with increased comprehension. Because this is the beginning of the year, you'll want to do a little work in each aspect of fluency, thus building a foundation of knowledge that you can draw on when coaching individual students during independent reading time.

On this fourth read, your students will be so familiar with the text that they will likely read through challenging words and phrases with relative ease. As you shift the focus to fluency, you may choose to pay particular attention to parsing—breaking sentences into meaningful phrases. As readers move into levels K, L, and M, the sentences they read become longer and more complex. These longer sentences require that readers know how to break sentences into meaningful parts and then understand not only what each part means but also how each part relates to the others. You will likely see children struggling with longer sentences in writing as well as reading. In writing time, many of your students are likely writing run-on sentences as they attempt to mimic the increased complexity of the sentences they are reading. Taking time in shared reading to study these longer sentences—how they work and what they mean—can support your students across the school day.

Reading pace is another important aspect of fluency for the beginning of the year. You are introducing reading logs during reading workshop, and you will likely have children setting reading goals. Through studying your students' logs over time, you will get a sense of who is reading too fast and who is reading too slowly. Shared reading is a great opportunity for the class as a whole to get used to reading at a quick but steady pace. When students seem to slow down or mumble over passages in shared reading, take the opportunity to reread, making the reading smoother and more comprehensible.

Of course, you'll want today's read to sound great, too! Be sure to get students actively looking for and using the prosodic cues that tell them how their reading should sound. Point out punctuation and font characteristics (bold, italics, all caps, enlarged print, words that sit alone on a line) and then prompt kids to match their voices accordingly. This work should be fun, but it should also give children a chance to put words to all these features and grow a stronger understanding of why authors use them in their texts. Finally, you'll want children to recall that the story itself often informs how we read a part. Have children play with rereading one sentence a few ways, thinking about which way best matches the mood, or feeling, of the story.

DAY FOUR FOCUS

✔ Reading with fluency (appropriate pacing, parsing, and prosody)

✔ Drawing attention to different types of punctuation, both mid- and end-of-sentence punctuation

✔ Reading for meaning

GETTING READY

✔ Display a copy of the song you used yesterday. Here we sing "There Was an Old Lady Who Swallowed a Fly" (see Warm Up).

✔ Prepare to share a chapter from the familiar text you read yesterday with students. Here we reread Chapter 3 from *Mercy Watson to the Rescue* (see Fourth Reading).

✔ Pull out a level J chapter book that you can read a few lines from to students (see Fourth Reading).

✔ Have ready a level L text with long sentences and Wikki Stix that students can use to break long sentences into meaningful phrases, or prepare a long sentence about *Mercy Watson to the Rescue* for students to practice punctuating (see After Reading).

WARM UP: *"There Was an Old Lady Who Swallowed a Fly"*

Sing the song, working to sing at a quick but steady pace throughout.

As you sing "There Was an Old Lady Who Swallowed a Fly" today, put an added emphasis on singing with a steady rhythm. Challenge students to sing smoothly throughout. This will be tricky when the phrases get longer and longer. To support students with this work, you might take a moment to talk through where you will break the sentences apart, and then try them a few ways—sometimes with shorter phrases and sometimes with longer phrases—until the singing is smooth.

FOURTH READING: *Mercy Watson to the Rescue*, Chapter 3, by Kate DiCamillo

Point out the longer sentences in the shared reading text and invite children to think about where they will take a breath.

Most texts at level A–J (and even many at K) are parsed out for the reader. That is to say, the reader can read to the end of each line of print, take a breath, and then read the next line, and the text will hold its meaning. This is something you might choose to point out to students today.

Pull out any level J chapter book and read a few lines together. Help kids to see that even when the sentence doesn't end at the end of the line, the *phrase* does. Next, pull out *Mercy Watson to the Rescue*. Turn to a page that has some longer sentences that wrap from line to line—page 16, for example. Read the text the same way, taking a long pause at the end of each line. The reading will make little sense, and you can all have a good laugh.

After this little demonstration, you can explain that as books get harder, the publishers no longer break up the sentences for you. You might say, "Now that you are growing as readers, you'll need to look for clues that will help you know where to take a breath in these longer sentences. Readers often look for middle-of-the-sentence punctuation to help them know when to take a breath. Let's notice some of that punctuation now. When my pointer touches any punctuation, will you put up a stop sign? Then we will name that punctuation mark and say if we will stop (for ending punctuation) or pause (for mid-sentence punctuation)." Practice only a page or two this way.

When your students put up their stop signs, make sure to comment on how each mark will affect your reading. You might say, "Wow! That period is in the middle of the line, but we will need to make a full stop there." Or, "Oh, that is a comma, so we should pause just a little bit, the way you would between reading items in a list." If children do not stop you, be sure to point out the punctuation they are missing.

Reread the text with students, and use your pointer to help children find a not-too-fast, not-too-slow pace for sections of the text.

By the fourth read, you will likely know the passages where your class starts to speed through the words. Sometimes this will happen because one part of the text is particularly exciting. As you near such a section of text, you might pause readers to say, "I know this next part is fun, but sometimes you read it so fast, I can't quite understand everything that is happening. Today as we read this part, I am going to run my pointer under the words. Will you read along with the pointer so that your reading is not too fast and not too slow?" This is work that you might choose to repeat in other sections of text where children are slowing down too much.

Of course, you may also notice in the moment of reading that children are reading one portion at an uneven rate. You can use your pointer to help them reread and regulate speed. Remember, though, pointing under the words too often will provide too much support. When children follow your pointer all the time, they do not develop the skill of tracking print with their eyes from one line to the next. Keep the pointer running along smoothly, making certain *not* to stop at each individual word, so that children read smoothly and fluently.

Make sure that students read with expression, too, by paying attention to font characteristics and what is happening in the text.

Working on parsing and pace will likely have a positive effect on your students' intonation, too. Breaking sentences into parts helps students stress words in meaningful ways, which lets the larger meaning of the text shine through. Just as you have given students a chance to notice the punctuation, give them the opportunity to notice and use font characteristics (bolds, italics, all caps, enlarged print) as well.

Remind your readers that the author puts all of these clues in the text to help them figure out how the book *wants* to be read. You might go on to add, "But you also need to use what's happening to help you know how to read the words!" Then have children think about how to read a sentence or two, letting the meaning of the words and their font characteristics guide their intonation. The sentences at the top of page 17 will provide a good opportunity for this.

> *Mercy recalled her lovely toast-filled dream.*
>
> *She wondered if there was any toast in the kitchen.*
>
> *While Mr. Watson and Mrs. Watson were arguing, Mercy hopped off the bed.*

You can lead the children in reading this once and then discussing how it wants to be read. You might even have them think a bit about which words in the passage should be stressed. For example, children might decide to slowly say the word *lovely* to give the sentence a dreamy effect or they might decide that *hopped* should be said quickly and with a high lilt to mimic the ease with which Mercy jumped from the bed.

AFTER READING

Invite students to experiment with parsing by breaking long sentences into meaningful phrases or adding punctuation.

A fun way to close this lesson is to give the children a chance to practice parsing with partners. You can pull a page from another text with long sentences (perhaps another level K or L text) for children to use in their practice. After you read the passage once together, you might have students put Wikki Stix on the page to show where one meaningful phrase ends and a new one begins. Then, together as a class, you can practice reading the page in the way that students think it should be read.

Another quick extension for this day could include displaying a long sentence for children to punctuate. You might write on a sentence strip a sentence that's hard to read and make sense of without the help of punctuation. For example, you could write something like this:

> *Mercy Watson to the Rescue a book for children was written in 2009 by author Kate DiCamillo winning her the hearts of many young readers*

Let the kids try out different punctuation to make this sentence sound right and make sense, each time practicing reading the sentence with the new punctuation.

DAY FIVE: Orchestration and Comprehension

Today, you will want to use your time during shared reading to celebrate the significant work students have done reading and rereading the text. Because of this, we suggest you allow the class to lead this final read, orchestrating all they have learned across this week. You will likely also want to use this time to grow students' comprehension, and we recommend you support students in considering how each part of the chapter they reread today connects with earlier and later parts of the story. We suggest you keep the conversations about this brief while students are reading, since you will have a significant amount of time for students to talk after reading today.

The fifth day of any shared reading experience with a text is a lovely time to engage students in a longer conversation about the text. Here, we recommend you use familiar structures from read-aloud to hold a grand conversation about how different parts of the text connect to one another.

Your role in this conversation will be one of facilitator. This means that you will need to make sure that the students are talking to each other, not to you. During the conversation, you can make your role clear by sitting outside the talk circle. Instead of responding to each student's ideas and comments, you can nudge students to say more by reminding them to use the text and other classroom tools. For example, we suggest you lift the level of the conversation by projecting specific parts of the text as students mention them and by displaying the talk chart you are using in read-aloud.

When the conversation comes to a close, you can quickly retell the main points children made, and then you'll likely want to end the week's work by adding copies of the shared reading text to the classroom library so students can borrow them to read.

DAY FIVE FOCUS

✔ Reading for deeper comprehension—thinking about how the chapter fits with the whole book

GETTING READY

✔ Display a copy of the song you used yesterday. Here we sing "There Was an Old Lady Who Swallowed a Fly" (see Warm Up).

✔ Prepare to share a chapter from the familiar text you read yesterday with students. Here we reread Chapter 3 from *Mercy Watson to the Rescue* (see Final Reading).

✔ Display the "Readers TALK about Books" chart from your read-aloud (see After Reading).

WARM UP: *"There Was an Old Lady Who Swallowed a Fly"*

Sing the song one more time, focusing on fluency.

Today's read should feel like a celebration of the week's work. You might start today's read by asking children to reflect on what they have learned, saying, "Readers, let's make our last read of this song the best yet! To do this, you'll need to remember *all* of the ways we have practiced this week. Take a minute now to think about our work, and when you think of something we should be sure to remember in our last read, put a thumb up!"

Then you can have readers share their thoughts in partnerships, before sharing a few ideas with the whole class. This will give students a moment to reflect on the skills that they have practiced before they employ them in this final read. Then let them sing their hearts out!

FINAL READING: *Mercy Watson to the Rescue*, by Kate DiCamillo

Encourage children to notice parts of this chapter that connect to parts in other chapters. Then reread the text with students, letting them lead the reading.

Since you have spent this week focused on one chapter of a longer book, today you might choose to have children start to think about how this chapter fits with the book as a whole. A great deal of the comprehension work readers need to do at the beginning of second grade centers on thinking across a book, so you'll want to seize the opportunity to practice that here.

You might say, "Readers, you all have been working so hard to read and think about this chapter this week. Today I thought we could think about how this chapter fits with the *rest* of the story. I know you have noticed things in this chapter that set us up for what happens later in the book. There are some things in this chapter that also connect with things that happened earlier in the book. Today as we read, will you put up a thumb when you notice something that connects to another part of the book? Then we can talk about the *whole* book at the end!"

As you read through the text, you might need to model a bit. After reading page 12, you might say, "Oh yes, this part really goes with what happened before. Look at this page from the last chapter. It says, 'They were so busy dreaming that they did not hear the floor moan.' And now in our chapter, the floor is breaking." This short model of connecting pages and parts will encourage children to do the same.

When you notice that a few children have ideas about connections, give students a moment to turn and talk. You can say, "Wow! It seems that a lot of you are noticing that this part connects to another part in the book. Will you all chat with a partner and think about another part this page goes with?" Make these turn-and-talks brief, because children will have more time to talk in a grand conversation after the read.

Because students are now quite familiar with the text, they are ready to take the lead in the final read. Read quietly, allowing students' voices to dominate today's rereading. Of course, you'll want this last read to be the most fluent yet. Make sure you continue to coach the reading so that the pace and intonation are strong.

AFTER READING

Reposition the class for a whole-class conversation, and channel students to retell the text prior to the start of the conversation.

Today you'll likely choose to end your shared reading time with a whole-class conversation. Ask the children to sit in a circle to ensure that they look at *and talk to* each other, rather than facing you as they talk. Before you begin the conversation, you might choose to have children retell the chapter to a partner. This will ensure that they are getting repeated practice with retelling and that everyone has a clear understanding of what happened in the chapter.

Display your discussion chart to set up for the whole-class conversation, and invite students to talk about connected parts in the text.

This conversation will progress in the same way your read-aloud conversations do, so you will want to read through the "Readers TALK about Books" chart (from Read-Aloud Session 2) before kicking off the conversation. Be sure to sit just to the outside of the circle and then offer a focus for the conversation. You might say, "As you read this chapter today, you noticed *so many* parts that connected to other parts in the book. Let's talk about some of those. Let's start with one person's idea and see if you can say lots and lots about how that one page goes with other parts in the story. Who wants to suggest a page to talk about first?" Call on one child to start the conversation, and then display the page she suggests on the document camera so that everyone can see.

After the first child offers her idea, wait for others to add on. The conversation might not last long just yet. After all, this is hard work. For now, focus your teaching primarily on getting students to talk to each other rather than directing all of their comments to you. If moving out of the circle has not solved this problem, try looking down or at the text when children talk, rather than meeting their gaze. You can also point to the chart called "Readers TALK about Books" and nod toward other children who might add into the conversation. The simple sentence, "Who has more to add?" can also help children keep their focus on each other while keeping the conversation going.

Once the children have talked as much as they can about one page and how it relates to the rest of the text, let someone else offer up a new part to discuss. You may end up discussing one part after another, or you may find that your students have lots to say about just one or two parts.

When the conversation has reached its end, make a big deal of returning the book to the library, thus making it available to anyone who want to read it *again*.